BLOC POLITICS
in the UNITED NATIONS

BLOC POLITICS
in the UNITED NATIONS

THOMAS HOVET, JR.

HARVARD UNIVERSITY PRESS
CAMBRIDGE, MASSACHUSETTS 1960

TO ERICA

ACKNOWLEDGMENTS

This book was initially prepared as a paper for the United Nations Project of The Center for International Studies, Massachusetts Institute of Technology. I am especially grateful to Dr. Lincoln P. Bloomfield, director of the project, whose confidence and patience made it possible for me to undertake the study. Particular thanks are due Mr. Richard W. Hatch, Editor-in-Chief at the Center, whose editorial guidance was invaluable. Thanks also to Professor Joseph Tanenhaus of New York University who was extremely helpful in formulating my ideas on the methodology of the study.

My initial interest in the study of international organization in general, and the United Nations, in particular, was influenced by Professor Linden A. Mander of the University of Washington and the late Professor Clyde Eagleton of New York University who gave me the basis of preparation for study in this field. Actually many of the ideas in this study are the result of a continuing interest and research about the General Assembly over a period of years. I was stimulated in my interest in this area when I worked with the International Studies Group of the Brookings Institution on their United Nations Project. My interest has been given continuous encouragement by Professor Waldo Chamberlin, who was my professor in graduate school and my supervisor with the Brookings Institution, and who is my colleague at New York University. To Professor Chamberlin I owe a debt for inspiration, guidance, and consultation which I can never repay. In the past my research on blocs in the United Nations has been helped by a grant from the faculty research fund of the Graduate School of Arts and Science of New York University. Throughout the years the assistance of the staff and facilities of the United Nations Documents Collection of New York University Library have helped my research. Lastly, none of my research and interest in this subject would have been realistic except for the help and assistance given by the many individuals in Delegations to the United Nations, as well as members of the U.N. Secretariat, who have to remain anonymous by their request. Naturally any faults in the study are entirely my responsibility and should in no way reflect upon any of the persons mentioned above.

16 October 1959   THOMAS HOVET, JR.
New York, N.Y.

CONTENTS

CHARTS

FOREWORD

Mr. Hovet's book was originally prepared as a contribution to the United Nations Project of the Center for International Studies, M.I.T. That project had as its purpose an evaluation of the uses of the United Nations over the next few years from the standpoint of broad United States and free world foreign policy objectives. Our general approach called for two kinds of analyses: a spelling out of broad strategic goals in order that the potential uses of the United Nations might be intelligibly tested; and an analysis of trends in the political processes of the international institution itself so that our vision of the present and, where possible, the future, might be informed with both reality and perception.

With the conviction that the formation of the negotiating and voting blocs in the United Nations was one of the most significant developments in its institutional history, we turned to Professor Hovet for what we hoped would be a definitive analysis of that phenomenon at its present stage of development. Mr. Hovet had access to a uniquely comprehensive collection of statistics on United Nations votes maintained at New York University and was highly knowledgeable as to their use and application. The result, I believe, is the most comprehensive and penetrating analysis thus far made of this important development in international politics.

It has become a truism that the complexion of political forces within the United Nations merely reflects the larger constellations of forces outside its walls. There is a world-wide trend toward consolidation and in some cases integration of formerly isolated political entities. It is not yet one world, but neither is it just two worlds — or for that matter eighty-two worlds — which a national policy must take into consideration. It is several worlds, each reflecting some degree of interdependence and common action on the basis of common interests, whether they be geographical, economic, or military. It is hardly surprising that within the United Nations these groupings should have rather quickly become explicit.

To be sure, each state is considered a single juridical entity in the eyes of international law. But the reality is rather in the alliances, the regional associations, the common markets, and the emerging federations. This book is the story of those groupings as they play their roles within the United Nations. It suggests some useful lessons for multilateral American diplomacy. But perhaps its most illuminating lesson is an implicit one which we should have learned earlier than we did: no sound program of peaceful cooperation can afford to neglect the truth that the political process — including the politics of blocs — is going to characterize man's efforts to govern himself at each and every level, whether ward, town meeting, state, nation, international organization — or world government.

October 20, 1959   LINCOLN P. BLOOMFIELD, *Director*
                          United Nations Project,
                          Center for International Studies,
                          Massachusetts Institute of Technology

BLOC POLITICS
in the UNITED NATIONS

▌ HISTORY AND METHOD

The present study is addressed to a development which has a new importance on the international scene, although the operation of bloc politics in the United Nations is not, of course, in itself a new phenomenon. It will be recalled that the practice of determining the allocation of elective seats on the United Nations' Councils by negotiation between interests in the General Assembly had its beginnings in the League of Nations, and that in the League of Nations Assembly, from the very beginning, states began to group themselves largely on the basis of geographical location and with regard to some political and economic factors.

The several blocs or groups in the League Assembly were: (1) the Latin American countries; (2) the United Kingdom and the Dominions; (3) the Scandinavian states, which were often joined with the Netherlands, and later Belgium and Switzerland; (4) France and the Little Entente; (5) Germany, Austria, Hungary, and Italy in the later stages; and (6) a series of less defined groupings of the Balkan states. These blocs or groups in the League Assembly were not wholly geographical because of the fact that for the most part League membership was confined to Europe, Latin America, and the British Dominions. Further, because of the unanimity rule and therefore the lack of the necessity to obtain a majority of supporters, the action of these groups was primarily limited to cooperation in electing members of the group to the Council and the smaller committees.

The lobbying of these groups gradually became more pronounced as the General Committee of the League Assembly became more political in character and it became imperative from the point of view of the groups that they have adequate representation on this Committee. In the first fifteen years of the League the Secretariat played a prominent role in preparing the "slate of elections" and in trying to work out successful compromises for all the groups. Discontent over the extent of lobbying led the Secretary-General of the League to make a plea before the First Committee of the Assembly in 1936 to find a way to mitigate this action, which he felt was causing unnecessary conflict. This concern finally led to a Norwegian proposal for a Nominations Committee, which was "to diminish the influence of the Secretariat in elections of the Assembly, and to increase the influence of the small powers upon the choice of the General Assembly." The League's use of this Committee was confined to the three Assemblies before the Second World War, but

> it worked well in the double sense of affording a message of democratic control and at the same time a measure of protection of the Secretariat, which must always, in the nature of the case, exercise considerable responsibility when it is a question of securing the difficult and delicate equipose, over a period of years, as between competence, and representation of nations and regions, with due regard also for political realities connected with the power and influence of particular states.[1]

It should be noted, however, that while the League Assembly's Nominations Committee took the pressure off the Secretariat, it might well have itself become the center of lobbying had not it been for the fact that by the time the Committee was created the importance of the League was already beginning to diminish and the political importance of elections along with it.

Since the League experience suggests that any organization based on majority decisions rather than unanimous decisions might well find bloc and group action prevalent in substantive matters as well as in elections, it may seem remarkable that in the planning stages of the United Nations there seems to have been no consideration of the consequent likelihood of the formation of blocs and groups. Neither at the Dumbarton Oaks discussions nor at the United Na-

---

[1] United Nations Preparatory Commission, Executive Commission, Subcommittee 1. *Memorandum by the Secretariat of Committee 1: Nominating Procedures in Major International Organizations*, Doc. PC/EX/A/23, 22 September 1945.

tions Conference on International Organization at San Francisco was any consideration given to the fact that an assembly operating on a majority decision basis would probably develop an informal structure of groups and blocs. The only allusion at the San Francisco Conference to the possibility of blocs and groups or to the implications of "bloc voting" was in a meeting of the Steering Committee (Chairmen of all the Delegations) when Mr. Molotov of the Soviet Union discussed the majority voting procedure of the conference.

He pointed out that the twenty votes of the American Republics, and the votes of Liberia and the Philippines, would constitute a bloc which would command nearly a majority of the votes in the Conference. He referred to the plenary session on April 30 at which twenty-eight votes had been cast against the motion of the Soviet Union, including the twenty votes of the American republics and eight votes of non-American countries, and he asked whether, in view of this situation, a simple majority voting arrangement would be likely to insure harmonious cooperation.[2]

There were several reasons why the experience of the League was not viewed with concern at the San Francisco Conference in considering the creation of a General Assembly operating with a majority decision type of voting procedure.

In the first place, the Security Council was conceived as the most important body of the new United Nations; with the voting procedure in the Council giving a veto to the permanent members, there was little concern that any bloc or group action would have an effect in the Council. In 1945, too, there was no realization of the fact that the membership of the United Nations would expand as a result of the independence of former colonial territories on the scale that has developed since that time. Not only was the Assembly's future role not conceived at the 1945 Conference, but also there was little conception of the extent to which the former colonial territories would be concerned with economic development and colonial problems in the Assembly. There seems to have been little aware-

[2] *Documents of United Nations Conference on International Organization* (New York: United Nations Information Organization, 1945), V, 175, Doc. 50, ST/2, p. 3.

ness of the extent to which the organization, enlarged by these newly independent states, would become immersed with issues arising as a result of the provisions of Chapter XI of the Charter regarding non-self-governing territories.

Also, of course, there was apparently little foresight in 1945 of the profundity of the tensions between the United States and the Soviet Union which have since dominated the world scene. Even had the United States foreseen the full extent of friction with the Soviet Union, without a parallel conception of the extent to which the number of states would be increased by newly independent areas, the United States would possibly not have been alarmed at the possibility of bloc and group developments since it might have anticipated support from the very groups that Mr. Molotov viewed with such alarm.

The San Francisco discussions on the election of members to the Councils did give an indication that there would be contests for the small number of elective seats. But even this did not seem a major problem in 1945 because of the fact that fairly adequate representation of the various interests appeared possible with an initial membership of only fifty-one. Nonetheless, when the matter was considered in the London meetings of the United Nations Preparatory Commission which followed the San Francisco Conference, considerable attention was given to procedures that might ease the election pressures. After prolonged discussion both in the Executive Committee and the Preparatory Commission itself, efforts to agree upon the creation of a nominations committee failed and the proposal was finally dropped.

The role that the General Committee of the Assembly was to exercise as a small "executive" body was subjected to even more extensive consideration. Inherent in the consideration of the role of the General Committee was the problem of its membership and how this was to reflect the various interest groups in the General Assembly. Even though the issue was resolved by the Preparatory Commission, it appeared again in the First Part of the First Session of the General Assembly when the question of the rules of procedure recommended by the Preparatory Commission were up for adoption by the Assembly. Similarly, consideration of the elements to be weighed in elections to the Security Council, the Economic and Social Council, the Trusteeship Council, and the International Court of Justice were discussed in the "preparatory stage" but to a much lesser degree than the question of the composition of the General Committee.

The question of the distribution of seats on the General Committee and the elected seats on the three councils was solved by an unwritten "gentleman's agreement" in behind-the-scenes negotiations during the meetings of the First Part of the First Session in London in 1946. The "agreement" was referred to as providing "geographical distribution," but in essence it constituted a recognition of the interest groups then discernible in the General Assembly. For example, the commonly noted "gentleman's agreement" on the election of the six non-permanent seats on the Security Council provided for two from Latin America, one from Eastern Europe, one from Western Europe, one from the Middle East, and one from the British Commonwealth.

From subsequent discussions in other sessions of the Assembly, it is arguable that the "one seat from Eastern Europe" was not to mean Eastern Europe in a geographical term, but Eastern Europe in the sense of the Soviet satellites, and certainly the one seat from the British Commonwealth was not from a geographical area. By not openly determining the interest groups that needed representation, but justifying the distribution of the seats on a nebulous kind of "geographical distribution," a basis was laid for the necessity of bloc and group organization and for negotiation between the blocs and groups so as to satisfy each "interest" group that it was being given adequate representation on the councils and in the all-important General Committee of the Assembly. Further, the fact that the initial agreement for the Security Council, for example, provided no seats for Asia east of Iran except through the British Commonwealth seat meant that organization of blocs and groups for this area was inevitable as the membership of the organization expanded from the original 51 to the present 82, largely through the increase in the number of Asian members.

In a very real sense, then, an important initial factor in the development of blocs and groups is to be found in the necessity of organizing coalitions of "interest" of sufficient strength to assure that each bloc or group would have as many seats on the councils and the General Committee as it could possibly obtain. The Security Council provides the simplest example of the problems posed by the initial "gentleman's agreement" and the vying of interests that have distorted it.

The table below indicates the non-permanent membership of the Security Council arranged in relation to those seats which were succeeded to by other members in accord with the initial "agreement" year by year (the non-permanent members being elected for two year terms).

Year	Latin America	Latin America	British Common-wealth	Western Europe	Eastern Europe	Middle East
1946	Brazil	Mexico	Australia	Netherlands	Poland	Egypt
1947	Brazil	Colombia	Australia	Belgium	Poland	Syria
1948	Argentina	Colombia	Canada	Belgium	Ukraine	Syria
1949	Argentina	Cuba	Canada	Norway	Ukraine	Egypt
1950	Ecuador	Cuba	India	Norway	Yugoslavia	Egypt
1951	Ecuador	Brazil	India	Netherlands	Yugoslavia	Turkey
1952	Chile	Brazil	Pakistan	Netherlands	Greece	Turkey
1953	Chile	Colombia	Pakistan	Denmark	Greece	Lebanon
1954	Brazil	Colombia	New Zealand	Denmark	Turkey	Lebanon
1955	Brazil	Peru	New Zealand	Belgium	Turkey	Iran
1956	Cuba	Peru	Australia	Belgium	Yugoslavia	Iran
1957	Cuba	Colombia	Australia	Sweden	Philippines	Iraq
1958	Panama	Colombia	Canada	Sweden	Japan	Iraq
1959	Panama	Argentina	Canada	Italy	Japan	Tunisia

The table illustrates many of the problems that developed in the competition of the interest groups to assure their degree of representation. For example, Turkey has been considered both a representative of Eastern Europe and of the Middle East in interpreting the original agreement. Eastern Europe, originally meaning the system of Soviet satellites, has also included Yugoslavia, after its break out of the Soviet orbit, then Greece and Turkey, and finally Japan and the Philippines. The fight in the General Assembly over whether this "Eastern European" seat should become an Asian seat, after the sudden increase in Asian members of the United Nations, illustrates the contribution that such a procedural issue has made towards the development of organized blocs and groups in the Assembly. The following rather typical news item is a good example of the maneuvering involved in these election fights:

DEAL TO GIVE YUGOSLAVIA COUNCIL SEAT

Nation Is Expected to Be Voted in
Today; Soviet Backs Proposal

United Nations, N.Y., Dec. 19 (AP) — Russia today joined the United States, Britain and France in support of a deal to end a stalemate for a Security Council seat by electing Yugoslavia.

This was reported by diplomats as key regional groups caucused secretly and, for the most part, lined up with the plan.

The Assembly will meet Tuesday. Diplomatic sources said they were confident Yugoslavia would be elected and, if so, the Assembly will adjourn its 1955 session quickly.

The scheme produced last week by Assembly President José Maza of Chile is a gentleman's agreement for the election of Yugoslavia Tuesday, for Yugoslavia to resign from the Security Council late in 1956 after serving one year, and for the Philippines to be elected by the 11th Assembly next fall to complete the remaining year of a 2-year term on the Council.

Yugoslavia and the Philippines have fought more than two months for the non-permanent seat on the Council held by Turkey. This has been known as the Eastern European seat.

Poland first ran against the Philippines but was dropped early in the contest. The Philippines and Yugoslavia have slugged it out since Oct. 14 through the 35th ballot on Friday without result. . . .[3]

A glance at the records of the General Assembly provides many examples of prolonged voting on elections to the elected seats on the councils, many of which have altered the concept implied in the initial "gentleman's agreement." Thus it is apparent that these understandings if they do exist, have been adjusted and altered as the

[3] *Washington Post*, 20 December 1955.

composition of the Assembly has been shifted not only by increases in the total membership, but also by the more particular organization of the interests within the Assembly into blocs and groups, a development which has made it possible for small states to exert an influence far out of proportion to either their population or their political importance when they combine their voting strength on particular issues.

Some have deplored the development of blocs. Addressing the General Assembly November 22, 1956, Mr. Cooper, delegate from Liberia, observed:

We come to the conference table with fixed ideas and immovable positions. Having formed ourselves into blocs in order to protect or foster some mode of life peculiar to our environment, or to enhance our position in world affairs, our stand becomes inflexible. The Organization, instead of being united, is now shattered into blocs which seem to be losing all power of cohesion. Such compacts appear not only to have paralyzed the Organization's decisions, but also to have penetrated the operation of the Organization itself, making it difficult for the Organization to work smoothly. Offices, memberships on committees, seats on various subsidiary organizations are all apportioned according to the strength of nations and the size of each bloc. In such conditions, no nation can afford to stand aloof, basing its interests upon right and justice. To exist in such conditions, it becomes not only necessary but imperative for a state to align itself with the group in which it thinks its interest may be best served and safeguarded. In such a situation, it is difficult to achieve solutions of world problems.[4]

Others would agree with Mr. Pinard, Canadian delegate, who, addressing the same session of the General Assembly two weeks later, said:

Increasingly, also we are dividing ourselves as Members of the United Nations into smaller groups. I think that this is in many respects a healthy phenomenon. It can be a partial solution to the problem of size. . . . When there is not time to hear every voice, there is a good deal to be

[4] United Nations. General Assembly. Eleventh Session. *Official Records. Plenary Meetings* (590th meeting, 22 November 1956), p. 244. Hereafter cited as UN.GA.XI. *OR.Plenary.*

said for choirs. Most of our groups, moreover, are not hard blocs. They are flexible and they are fortunately, not exclusive. It is only natural and fitting that like-minded countries should work together; but it is neither natural nor fitting when a group is forced to become — superficially, at least — so united that it automatically votes as one, on even the most unimportant procedural issues. Fortunately for the work of our organization, there is only one such bloc — and even here there have of late been hopeful signs of restless intelligence at work.[5]

But the important thing about such views is not their divergence. It is their common recognition of a political phenomenon which James Madison recognized in the *Federalist* more than a hundred years ago as an inevitable feature of representative political bodies, and which, by the very nature of the United Nations organization, has assumed an emphatic role in the conduct of the General Assembly.

By the terms of the United Nations Charter the General Assembly is the only principal organ consisting of all the members (Art. 9, par. 1); it may discuss almost any question and make recommendations (Art. 10); and each member of the General Assembly has one vote, decisions being made by either a simple or two-thirds majority (Art. 18). In addition to its broadly representative nature, the fact that the Assembly is not a true legislative body empowered to pass bind-ing resolutions but can only recommend courses of action to the members encourages alliances since they can be entered into with-out any great sense of responsibility. This point was emphasized by the New Zealand Representative, Sir Carl Berendsen, when he said in the Second Session:

No one in this room can deny — no one in this room will deny — that there has been in the General Assembly, to quote the leader of the Indian delegation, some huckstering of votes in the marketplace. I do not, of course, mean that votes are bought for money. But votes are indeed bought and paid for with other votes — "You vote for me in this matter, and I will vote for you in that." Votes that are bargained for in that way are not cast responsibly according to the merits of the matter under consideration. That is no way to cast a vote.[6]

[5] UN.GA.XI. *OR. Plenary.* 609th mtg., 5 December 1956, pp. 538–539.
[6] UN.GA.II. *OR.Plenary.* 167th mtg., 3 November 1947, p. 695.

Five years later Sir Carl felt that this element of irresponsibility was still present in the Assembly. In a speech reflecting on his experience in the Assembly he said:

One deplorable aspect of the Assembly voting is intrigue and the hustling for votes in the lobbies and hotel rooms. Even on the most fundamental matters votes are bought and sold . . . by a system of bargaining which some think a part of the democratic system, but which I and many others, think disgusting and menacing.[7]

We would say that the members of the General Assembly are not acting "irresponsibly" in terms of their governments' objectives when concern for those objectives requires them to strike such voting bargains but, rather, as representatives in any parliamentary body. In the United States Congress the individual members, elected to represent the interests of their districts or states, have to consider those interests in their actions in Congress if they are to be politically successful in continuing in office. The real difference in the case of the General Assembly is that, since there are no binding decisions, members agreeing to vote for a resolution of no primary concern in exchange for votes on an issue of primary concern can undertake such commitments with a realization that essentially they have nothing more than a moral obligation to vote for and implement resolutions they thus support. In other words, the nature of the Assembly not only makes voting alliances necessary, but it makes them easier to achieve than in other parliamentary bodies.

This is especially important from the point of view of the more important members such as the United States. If a major power can recognize the interests of other and smaller members, and through its political and economic power help to implement the resolutions of real concern to these smaller states, it can work out arrangements which will provide adequate voting support for its views on the matters of its primary concern. The United Nations was in large part conceived on the basis that while there would be an equal vote for each member, it would be the major powers — the permanent mem-

[7] *Dominion* (Wellington, New Zealand), 19 June 1952.

bers of the Security Council — who would bear the primary responsibility for the maintenance of peace and security. Thus an alliance
of major powers can exert such influence as to ensure the success
of their policies in the Security Council; but in the Assembly such
success is not possible unless an understanding of the issues vital
to the smaller members is achieved as a basis for compromises that
can be worked out to mutual satisfaction. Thus the ease of forming
voting alliances presents ample opportunities for major powers.

Another constitutional factor in the development of blocs and
groups in the General Assembly is the fact that the Security Council,
the Economic and Social Council, and the Trusteeship Council are
organs with a limited membership, smaller than that of the United
Nations as a whole. For the concerns of these three smaller organs
are in some cases more vital to the members than the issues before
the Assembly, and if these organs are to be successful they must be
in effect microcosms not only of the total membership but of the
interests of the Assembly. It follows that each member of the Assembly has an important interest in seeing that these smaller bodies
represent so far as possible the membership as a whole — a natural
incentive to the formation of interest groups in the General Assembly
whenever there are elections to the other organs.

The steadily increasing membership of the United Nations, and
in particular the large increase in 1955 with the admission *en bloc* of
new members, has been a further factor in the organization and
development of blocs and groups. (The accompanying table indicates the number of members in each session according to *actual*
geographic area.)

Sessions	Asia	Africa	Americas	Europe	Australia
I(1)	9	4	22	14	2
I(2)	11	4	22	16	2
II	13	4	22	16	2
III	14	4	22	16	2
IV	15	4	22	16	2
V	16	4	22	16	2
VI	16	4	22	16	2

Sessions	Asia	Africa	Americas	Europe	Australia
VII	16	4	22	16	2
VIII	16	4	22	16	2
IX	16	4	22	16	2
X	21	5	22	26	2
XI	22	8	22	26	2
XII	23	9	22	26	2
XIII	22	9	22	26	2

The factors of common interest are so many and so interwoven that —
to give but one example — the Latin American states might be allied
with the United States in issues relating to the cold war but with the
new Asian and African states on matters of economic assistance to
underdeveloped countries.

Given the naturalness and apparent inevitability of the development of interest groupings in the political climate of the General
Assembly, a product of the United Nations Charter itself, and the
fact of the increasingly overt roles of groups in the Assembly, it is
unfortunate that there has been no systematic study of blocs and
other interest groups in the United Nations and that journalistic
comment has been so generalized as to contribute little to public
understanding of the extent and nature of this phenomenon. Clearly,
if the General Assembly is to serve a role as a successful political
organ in the international scene it is essential from the point of view
of the United States, as one of the major powers, that there be a
complete awareness of the nature and extent of bloc voting and
politics, and a sense of political sophistication of the factors that
have to be considered in pursuing policy objectives in such an atmosphere. Proper awareness of bloc politics in the General Assembly
by the United States can make that organ a useful diplomatic tool,
while a lack of awareness can mean that participation in the Assembly may more often than not result in diplomatic defeats and a loss
of world leadership before the forum of the world. If fact, if the
United States does not use the United Nations in general, and the
General Assembly in particular, as a major instrument of policy it
can well be because a lack of political sophistication prevents the

use of this bloc development in achieving policy aims. Any assumptions on the diplomatic tactics to be used to achieve the foreign policy objectives of the United States in the United Nations can only be realistically conceived if there is an awareness of both the useful and detrimental elements present in the General Assembly, from the point of view of the United States, as a result of the extent and nature of the bloc politics that exist in that body.

With the foregoing in mind, this monograph will attempt an over-all consideration of bloc or group politics in the General Assembly as well as an effort to relate these developments to the diplomatic policies and interests of the United States. Accordingly, this study embraces an over-all survey of the blocs and groups that have developed, an individual consideration of each of the blocs and groups, an examination of the combinations and coalitions of blocs and groups in the United Nations, and some conclusions on the role of the United States in relation to blocs and groups.

In general, blocs and/or groups will be defined as any political group of states operating as units in the General Assembly — ranging from those with formal organizations and binding commitments to those with no organization and only with like areas of interest — although more specific detailed "definitions" will be developed in the second section in making an over-all survey of the blocs and groups that have developed. In essence this study is concerned with trying to understand, by analysis, the full extent to which blocs or groups exist as hard and fast groups within the organization. It will also emphasize the cohesive and divisive factors within the blocs and groups as well as attempting to understand the extent of the likelihood of the formation of new groupings of states within the General Assembly.

The analysis is based largely on the *Official Records* and other documents of the United Nations, supplemented by various governmental documents and statements and the extensive secondary source material appearing in academic and popular journals and newspapers around the world; on interviews and conversations with officials of the United Nations and the various delegations to the United

Nations, as well as with certain outside observers; and on an examination of voting, primarily in the General Assembly.

Insofar as the use of documents and secondary source material is concerned these are cited directly only when they have been used for quotations. Information from interviews was received in most instances with the understanding that it would be used without attribution to individuals. The author's use of the record of voting in the General Assembly as a basis for analysis is explained in the following pages.

Since the most meaningful votes for the purposes of the present study are those in the organs in which all of the members of the United Nations are represented, the votes analyzed here are primarily those in the main committees and the plenary sessions of the General Assembly, although in some instances votes in smaller organs such as the General Committee and the Security Council are considered. From the time the General Assembly came into being in January 1946, there were at least 8,917 votes in the plenary and main committees through the thirteenth regular session ending in March 1959. Of this total, at least 6,184 votes [8] were held in the main committees and 2,733 votes in the plenary. Unfortunately for the purpose of analysis, only 1,908, or 21.6 per cent, of the votes were roll-call votes. Thus there is no *official* record of 78.4 per cent of the votes. However, since the roll-call votes were for the most part presumably on issues which some, or all, of the members considered important enough for one reason or another to request a roll call, one may not be too far off in considering that they provide a fairly accurate reflection of the voting patterns on "important" issues in the General Assembly. This latter point is partially substantiated by the fact that there were an almost identical number of roll-call votes in the plenary (22.8 per cent) and in the main committees (21.8 per cent), suggesting a similar number of matters important enough to lead to roll-call requests.

---

[8] "At least" because in the case of some of the main committees the *Official Records* are summary records and not verbatim records, and it is therefore difficult to be certain that all decisions by vote have been noted.

In addition to distinguishing *roll-call* votes, two other categories or types of votes might be indicated: *show-of-hands* and *adopted-without-objection* votes. *Show-of-hand* votes are those in which members indicated their vote by raising their hands for counting but which were recorded only in total figures without indicating how each member voted. The *adopted-without-objection* votes are those in which the Assembly agreed, in essence, by acclamation because there was no call for a *show-of-hands* or *roll-call* vote. These three types of votes are common to most parliamentary or legislative bodies.

As indicated above, for the most part roll-call votes generally constitute about 20 per cent of the votes, with the remaining 80 per cent being either show-of-hands votes or adopted-without-objection votes. There has been a definite trend toward more show-of-hands votes, accompanied of course by a diminishing number of adopted-without-objection votes (Chart A).[9] Thus there has been an increasing percentage of votes on which the members have been divided (i.e., the total percentage of roll-calls plus show-of-hands votes), indicating that roll-call votes have not necessarily included all the significant votes which must be considered in any "bloc voting" analysis, and that an evaluation of group and bloc coherence would have to include consideration of the show-of-hands votes as well as the roll-call votes. This poses a problem since there is no official tabulation of each member's vote on the show-of-hands votes. However, many delegations attempt to record the vote of individual

[9] To avoid confusion the percentages for the two special sessions and the three emergency special sessions have been left out of this and other charts for the most part, because percentages for these special sessions would be somewhat misleading in determining trends due to their special nature, the limited number of votes, and the fact that the items of concern in these sessions are not comparable with the matters of concern of the regular sessions. However, the *total* figures and the *total* percentages indicated in the text include all roll-call votes in the regular, special, and emergency special sessions. It should also be noted that the first regular session met in two parts, and each is considered as a regular session because they were almost a year apart, covered the whole range of matters of concern, and are thus comparable to the other regular sessions.

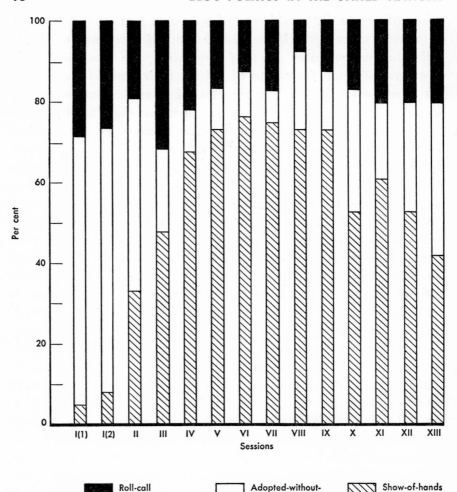

A. Types of votes in the plenary (per cent per regular session)

members on certain issues when the vote is taken by a show-of-hands, and several delegations, through the use of numerous "spotters," attempt to keep fairly detailed and complete records of all individual member votes when the show-of-hands procedure is used. Insofar as it has been possible to obtain delegation records they are considered in the analysis, especially in the instances where it was essential to go beyond the officially recorded roll-call votes in order to understand the precise issues evidencing cohesion or division within a group or bloc.

A further qualification in using roll-call votes as a "bloc voting" guide is the fact that not all the roll-call votes have been on *substantive* issues (i.e., votes on draft proposals, draft resolutions in whole or part); some have been on procedural issues (i.e., including items on the agenda, determining the question of a two-thirds majority requirement, motions to adjourn). One hundred and seventeen, or 6.1 per cent, of the 1,908 roll-call votes have been held on procedural issues, and 93.9 per cent have been concerned with substantive matters (Chart B). The lack of any trend in the percentage of roll-call procedural versus substantive votes would tend to indicate that a roll-call vote on a procedural issue is limited to important procedural issues, which in most cases are important matters bordering on being substantive issues. This hypothesis is borne out in examining the procedural roll calls, which show that most of the votes involve matters which are significant. For example, a procedural vote on whether to include an item like "the question of West Irian" on the agenda is almost as significant as a vote on the substantive aspects on the same issue. In fact, in some sessions when the General Assembly was not able to agree on any proposal or resolution on "the question of West Irian," the most significant vote may well have been the procedural decision to include the issue in the agenda.

If roll-call votes are to be used as a guide to "bloc voting" trends, the question remains whether *all* roll-call votes should be used or only an *adjusted gross*. If all were used many duplicate roll calls would be included, because most controversial issues are voted by roll call both in the main committees and in the plenary on the recommendation of the main committee, which raises the question as to the ratio of roll calls in the two committees (Chart C). While there is a variance session by session, 67.5 per cent of the 1,908 roll call votes were held in the meetings of main committees and 32.5 per cent in the plenary. A somewhat different percentage is ap-

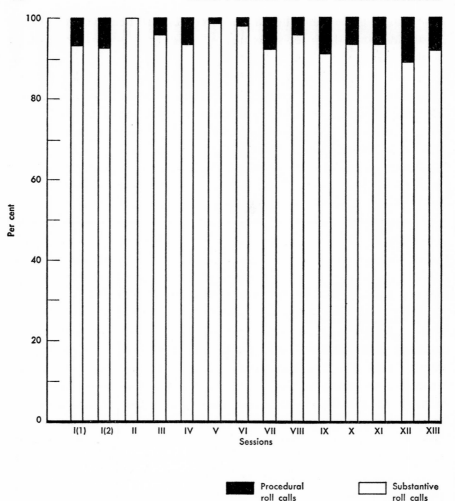

B. Substantive and procedural roll-call votes in the General Assembly (per cent per regular session)

parent in the case of procedural and substantive roll calls (Chart D). The reason for the higher percentage of total roll calls in the main committees is that there has been a greater number of substantive roll call votes, and, as Chart D indicates, 68.8 per cent of the substantive roll call votes are in the main committees. The higher

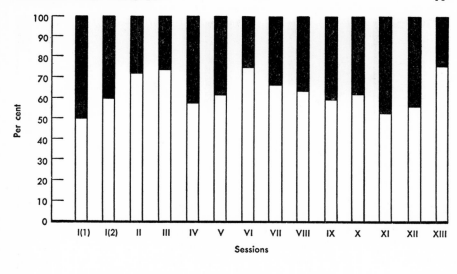

C. Number of roll-call votes in the main committees and plenary of the General Assembly (per cent per regular session)

number of substantive roll calls in the committee is explained by several facts. In the first place, many more draft proposals and amendments are submitted in the main committee discussions, and, if they are considered sufficiently important by their sponsors, there is a tendency to request a roll call vote. Secondly, examination of the debates in the *Official Records* reveals that there is a greater tendency in the main committees to have paragraph-by-paragraph votes on draft resolutions by roll calls whereas the practice in the plenary is to have a roll-call vote on the draft resolution as a whole or to have one or two roll-call votes on the key paragraphs. Thus there is a considerable duplication of roll-call votes, at least on key paragraphs, in the main committees and the plenary. On the other hand, in the case of the roll-call votes on procedural issues there tends to be little if any such duplication of votes. In the Assembly plenary many of the roll-call votes on procedural matters are votes on the inclusion of items in the agenda. In the main committees the majority of procedural votes are generally on issues relating to the

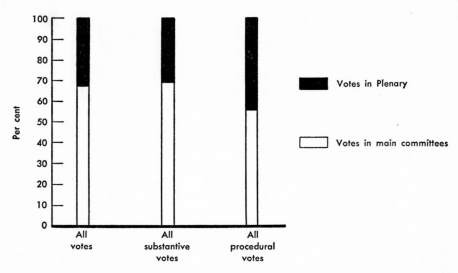

D. Number of roll-call votes on all votes, substantive votes and procedural votes cast in the main committees and the plenary of the General Assembly (by percentage)

sequence in which various draft proposals on a substantive issue should be considered, or on a motion to adjourn to allow for further consultations between delegations before proceeding to vote on the substantive proposals.

These facts on the extent of procedural and substantive roll calls in the main committees and the plenary are very pertinent to determining the extent of "bloc voting." If all 1,908 substantive and procedural roll-call votes are considered in assessing "bloc voting," the results will be distorted, especially if duplicate roll call votes in the main committees and the plenary have the same breakdown results. Therefore, in using a majority of the roll calls to assess "bloc voting" trends for our purposes an *adjusted* number of roll-call votes is used.

This *adjusted gross* number includes:

(1) *All substantive roll call votes in the plenary except those on issues which were overwhelmingly defeated in the main committee paragraph-by-paragraph, in which case only one plenary roll call will be included — the key paragraph vote which set the voting trend.* The plenary roll call will be used rather than the committee

votes because of the greater likelihood that all members will be present during voting in plenary session. Also, the plenary votes are the final votes for the record and are generally cast after the individual members have had sufficient time to reflect on their positions. With respect to substantive proposals which have been overwhelmingly defeated (i.e., by 3 to 1 or more) in committee, some sponsors often insist on paragraph-by-paragraph votes, which have no chance of reversal in the plenary, so that they can point out for propaganda purposes the dominance of particular group combinations in the Assembly. For the most part the Soviet Union and its satellites pursued this course of action in the earlier sessions, forcing as many as eighteen paragraph-by-paragraph roll-call votes on one of their "propaganda" proposals. If these votes in their entirety were included it would create an illusion of a greater degree of coherence on the part of other groups than might rightfully be said to exist. Thus only the key vote on "spite" resolutions is included in the *adjusted gross* roll-call votes. In later sessions of the Assembly this is not such a problem because, after a roll-call defeat on the key paragraph, the other paragraphs of the "spite" proposals were voted on by a show-of-hands procedure.

(2) *Substantive roll-call votes of the main committees which were overruled by the plenary.* In most cases these were votes on items which either received a bare majority in support or defeat, votes which were altered by a shift of the vote of several members in the Assembly plenary. In some instances these were votes which passed the main committees with a simple majority but which were defeated in the plenary because they were substantive matters requiring a two-thirds majority according to Article 18 of the Charter. The other roll calls on substantive matters in the main committees are excluded from the *adjusted gross* because of their duplication in the plenary; if they were included they would only accentuate and distort the indications of group and bloc cohesion or division.

(3) *Only the most important procedural roll calls in the main committees and plenary.* The important procedural roll calls have been determined by considering each in the context of the debates.

Generally, they include votes on placing a controversial item on the agenda, or on whether a particular draft resolution will be in the category which requires a two-thirds majority to pass.

On the basis of these three criteria, 521 roll-call votes (27.3 per cent) of the total of 1,908 roll calls have been included.

In addition to using an *adjusted gross* number of roll calls to assess the nature and extent of "bloc voting," in many instances the cohesion and division of blocs and groups have been assessed on the basis of what will be called *significant resolution* roll calls. Nine individuals, including members of several delegations, members of the Secretariat, and outside experts, were given the bound volumes of the Assembly resolutions and were asked to survey them session by session and to select approximately ten resolutions they considered the most significant in each regular session through the Twelfth Session (two or three in the case of special sessions). The nine individual lists were compared; there were 66 resolutions on which *all* the individuals agreed, and it is those resolutions which have been considered the *significant resolutions*. In consultation with these individuals, agreement was reached as to which plenary vote on each of these significant resolutions could be considered the key vote. The *significant resolution* "roll calls" therefore include the key plenary vote on each of the 66 *significant resolutions*. When there were only show-of-hands votes, the votes of individual members in the show-of-hands voting have been determined from "count records" compiled by several delegations. They are so indicated if they are discussed by individual resolution in considering the implications of the vote with regard to a particular group or bloc.

One final point needs to be made in connection with the use of "bloc voting" as a factor in determining trends of cohesion and division within groups or blocs. It is not sufficient simply to analyze the roll-call votes collectively; they also must be considered in relation to their subjects, and more especially in generalized subject categories, particularly if the analysis is to be used as a basis for contemplating future trends. This does not mean that votes should not be considered individually in relation to the specific issue and the special circumstances; rather, it means that if these particular issues are to be generalized upon for contemplating future trends they have to be organized into subject and type categories.

The General Assembly itself attempts to have related subject items considered in the initial stage — the main committee stage — in subject groups (i.e., administrative and budgetary matters are initially considered in the Fifth (Main) Committee). While there is a temptation to categorize the votes according to the main committees which considered the matter or referred it to the Assembly, this is not a realistic method. A resolution on "the question of persons of Indian origin in the Union of South Africa" may have resulted from discussions in the First Committee (political and security matters), but the resolution itself may simply create a commission to study the problem and therefore the resolution is not *in essence* concerned with either the substance of "pacific settlement" or "human rights" but is actually concerned with "structure" in that it created an organ. As another example, a resolution resulting from discussions in the Fifth Committee (administrative and budgetary matters) may establish precedents with respect to the position of international civil servants in such a way that it is really not an "administrative" matter but more in the category of "the development of international law." Another reason why categorizing votes according to the main committees and their subjects is considered impractical is that many resolutions result from the actions of the plenary directly without prior referral to a committee, or from consideration by committees other than the main committees. Chart E shows the number of resolutions eventually passed by the plenary according to their source of origin. This chart also indicates how many of those resolutions, from the different sources of initial consideration, were subject to roll call votes at some stage of their adoption. We see that 175 resolutions, or about 13.0 per cent of the total, were considered by either the plenary directly or committees other than the regular subject matter main committees. Even more important, 54 of these resolutions had roll call votes, which is 23.6 per cent of the total of 232 resolutions which were subjected to roll-calls. These facts imply that any categorization of roll call votes on the basis of the subject matter of the committees would be quite misleading.[10] A good many of the resolutions considered only in the plenary are very significant substantive ones, such as the resolutions on the Hungarian situation and the Suez intervention in 1956.

For our purposes, therefore, subject categories are determined on the basis of the subject of the resolution as revealed by its wording rather than on the basis of the committees which initially considered the issue. Using Article 1 of the Charter as a general guide of subject concerns of the United Nations, the subject resolutions (and related roll-call votes) have been categorized as follows:

(a) Collective measures, including such issues as regulations of armaments
(b) Peaceful settlement
(c) Self-determination
(d) Economic cooperation
(e) Social and cultural
(f) Humanitarian cooperation (i.e., relief and short-term social cooperation)
(g) Human rights
(h) Development of international law
(i) Administrative, procedural, and structural

The resolutions (and related roll calls) have also been categorized on the basis of the type of action they required regardless of subject, the attempt being to distinguish those resolutions which required implementation by the members. These categories are:

(a) States to supply funds
(b) States to supply information
(c) States to take other actions
(d) Other (i.e., referral to other organs, bodies, organizations; a general statement, etc.)

[10] A recent study which uses the main committee categorization of resolutions (and votes) for analysis is Robert E. Riggs, *Politics in the United Nations: A Study of United States Influence in the General Assembly* (Urbana: University of Illinois Press, 1958). The problems posed by such criteria are amply illustrated in this book, which although in many respects one of the most perceptive bloc studies of an academic nature, is limited to analyzing only 86 roll call votes.

Source of resolutions   Number of resolutions

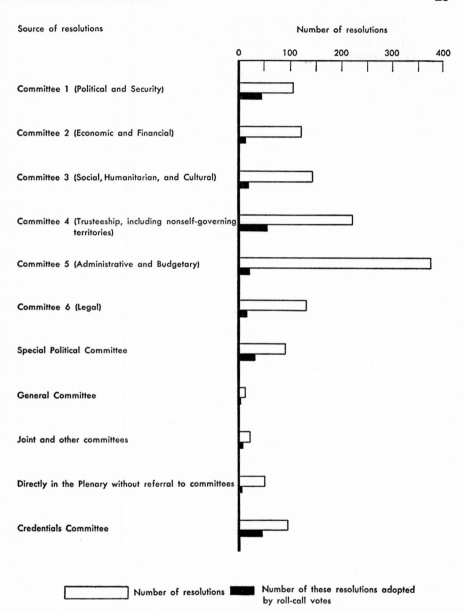

E. Number of resolutions passed by the United Nations General Assembly according to their source of origin, including an indication of how many of these resolutions were adopted by roll-call votes

While the breakdown of the resolutions and roll call votes into one or more of the categories of subject and type of action has been made by what is, in essence, a subjective process, the analysis was made in consultation with individuals in the Secretariat and in delegations and with outside experts. In cases where there might be argument as to the subject breakdown, the individual resolutions and roll calls alluded to in assessing bloc and group cohesion and division are individually identified.

It is apparent from the breakdown of resolutions according to source of initial (main committee) consideration (Chart E) that in certain areas there tends to be a higher number of roll call votes than in others. Thus, since from the Fifth Committee (administrative and budgetary) there were 370 resolutions, only 17, or 0.46 per cent, of which were subjected to roll-call votes, generalizations on votes from the Fifth Committee, at least on the basis of roll calls, are not so valid as in the case of First Committee (political and security), where 38.9 per cent of the resolutions had roll-call action. Of course, First Committee resolutions are of a more controversial nature and therefore subject to more requests for roll calls. Chart F indicates the percentage of resolutions on which there have been roll-call votes according to the subject categories which this monograph uses in its analysis.

This chart shows that the highest percentage of resolutions subjected to roll-call votes were resolutions concerned with what were administrative, procedural, and structural matters (26.3 per cent), followed in order of decreasing percentage by self-determination issues (23.0 per cent), peaceful settlement issues (18.5 per cent), collective measures issues (10.4 per cent), and human rights issues (9.4 per cent), with issues involving economic cooperation, social and cultural cooperation, humanitarian cooperation, and development of international law ranging from 1 per cent to 5 per cent. Thus the truly substantive issues most likely to evoke a roll-call request are self-determination, peaceful settlement, collective measures, and human rights. It would be misleading to assume that most roll-call concerns are with administration, procedure, and structure; the is-

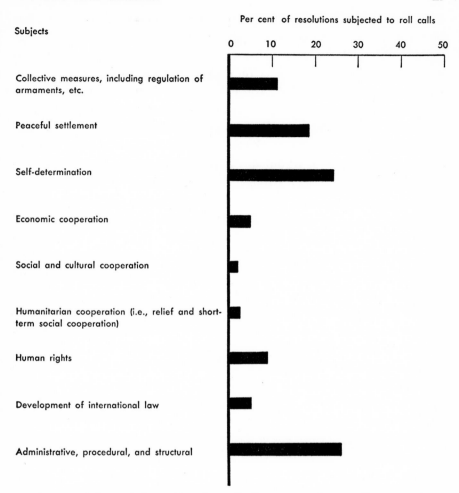

Per cent of resolutions subjected to roll calls

Subjects

| | 0 | 10 | 20 | 30 | 40 | 50 |

Collective measures, including regulation of armaments, etc.

Peaceful settlement

Self-determination

Economic cooperation

Social and cultural cooperation

Humanitarian cooperation (i.e., relief and short-term social cooperation)

Human rights

Development of international law

Administrative, procedural, and structural

F. Per cent of the resolutions subjected to roll-call votes according to subject categories

sues in this category are in their essence watered-down recommendations attempting to solve self-determination, peaceful settlement, and similar issues which resulted in no substantive decision except to refer the problem to another organ (procedure), to create a commission to study (structure), etc. Thus, the category of "administration, procedure, and structure" contains the weakest substantive types of resolutions even though they were concerned with matters

important enough to lead to roll-call votes. This chart also empha-
sizes that the validity of conclusions on "bloc voting" are more likely
to be accurate reflections of bloc and group cohesion and division
in the categories of subjects in which at least 10 per cent of the
resolutions were subject to roll-call voting than in the other categories where the number of resolutions is not really large enough
to give a valid sampling. It can also be argued that the subject
categories with larger percentages of resolutions with roll-call votes
represent the areas of significant and controversial concern.

II AN OVER-ALL VIEW OF BLOCS AND GROUPS

We have only to turn to the Official Records of the General Assembly of the United Nations to establish the very active presence of bloc politics as a constant factor in the operation of that world body. The connotations of the following samples from those records are unmistakable.

MR. MALOES (*Philippines*): As chairman of the African-Asian group, I want to bring a very important question to the Assembly. . . .[1]

MR. SPAAK (*Belgium*): [translated from French] I should first of all like to explain that I am speaking on behalf not only of my delegation, but also of those of the Netherlands and Luxembourg, the three Benelux countries having agreed to speak with one voice. . . .[2]

MR. DAVID (*Czechoslovakia*): [translated from Russian] It is a great honor for me to speak on behalf of the Eastern European countries. . . .[3]

MR. BANDARANAIKE (*Ceylon*): . . . I must tell the Assembly that it is my view, and the views of my colleagues, the other Asian Prime Ministers, that the position is still extremely delicate and dangerous. . . .[4]

MR. JAMALI (*Iraq*): . . . The Committee we propose should study with the representatives of the Asian-African group their complaints of injustice. . . .[5]

MR. URQUIA (*El Salvador*): [translated from Spanish] Two equally gratifying circumstances enable me to take the floor at this time . . . the second . . . circumstance is my position as chairman of the group of Latin American representatives accredited to the United Nations, with the consequence that I can speak on behalf of all my colleagues from that part of the world. . . .[6]

[1] UN.GA.XII. *OR. Plenary*, 679th mtg., 18 September 1957, p. 15.
[2] UN.GA.XI. *OR. Plenary*, 594th mtg., 24 November 1956, p. 295.
[3] UN.GA.XII. *OR. Plenary*, 690th mtg., 26 September 1957, p. 179.
[4] UN.GA.XI. *OR. Plenary*, 590th mtg., 22 November 1956, p. 232.
[5] UN.GA.XI. *OR. Plenary*, 628th mtg., 20 December 1956, p. 762.
[6] UN.GA.XI. *OR. Plenary*, 623rd mtg., 18 December 1956, p. 724.

Naturally, the development of this phenomenon has not gone un-noticed; and its operation has been discussed by political observers in what already constitutes a considerable body of comment.

However, the steady flow of such comment has been directed for the most part at specific instances of bloc organization and action and set in a general context of acceptance of the inevitability of bloc politics. There has been little or no attempt at systematic examination of the total phenomenon. As a result there is still much vagueness as to exactly what blocs and groups do exist in the General Assembly. Since many of them have similar names, they are often assumed to be one and the same when actually they are not. For example, it appears that the "Soviet bloc" and the "Eastern European group" are generally considered synonymous and identical although in fact they have slightly different memberships and roles in the Assembly. Moreover, as a result of the fact that the groups are flexible and many have overlapping memberships, one encounters not only confusion as to bloc and group identities but also only partial awareness of the full extent of the bloc and group structure in the General Assembly and the United Nations.

Thus the first step in any attempt to relate the operation of bloc politics in the United Nations to the effective participation of the United States in that world body must be to clarify the nature and extent of the bloc and group development in general.

Compared with the early years, the General Assembly of 1959 presents a fairly complicated structure of blocs and groups, the identities and extent of which can be best considered in terms of the following categories based on the roles they plan and the degree to which they are organized — or unorganized, as might be the case: blocs, caucusing groups, geographical distribution groups, regional organization groups, common interest groups, and temporary groups.

BLOCS

A *bloc* might best be defined as a group of states which meets regularly in caucus and the members of which are bound in their votes in the General Assembly by the caucus decision. Using this definition, there is present only one true *bloc* — the Soviet bloc, which to all intents and purposes operates as a single unit with nine votes, the number of its members.[7] The members of the Soviet bloc at the present time are: Albania, Bulgaria, Byelorussia, Czechoslovakia, Hungary, Poland, Rumania, Ukraine, and the Soviet Union.

In contrast to a *bloc*, the other "informal" political organizations in the Assembly are generally termed *groups*. There are several types of groups but all are distinguished from blocs by the fact that, although they share a common basis for consultation on issues, such consultation does not result in a decision which binds their members as to how they vote in the Assembly.

CAUCUSING GROUPS

The term *caucusing group* may be applied to any group of member states in the Assembly which has some degree of formal organization, holds fairly regular meetings, and is concerned with substantive issues and related procedural matters before the sessions of the General Assembly. (Thus the list below does not include such groups as the "old Commonwealth" and NATO which function on an *ad hoc* basis only.) As of 1959, there were eight caucusing groups in the General Assembly:

Asian-African group: 29 members — Afghanistan, Burma, Cambodia, Ceylon, Ethiopia, Ghana, Guinea, India, Indonesia, Iran, Iraq, Japan, Jordan, Laos, Lebanon, Liberia, Libya, Malaya, Morocco, Nepal, Pakistan, Philippines, Saudi Arabia, Sudan, Thailand, Tunisia, Turkey, United Arab Republic (Syria and Egypt), and Yemen

Arab group: 10 members — Iraq, Jordan, Lebanon, Libya, Morocco, Sudan, Saudi Arabia, Tunisia, United Arab Republic (Syria and Egypt), and Yemen

African group: 9 members — Egypt, Ethiopia, Ghana, Guinea, Liberia, Libya, Morocco, Sudan, and Tunisia

Benelux group: 3 members — Belgium, Luxembourg, and the Netherlands

[7] See the discussion on the Soviet bloc as a voting unit on pages 49–54.

Commonwealth group: 9 members — Australia, Canada, Ceylon, Ghana, India, Malaya, New Zealand, Pakistan, Union of South Africa, and the United Kingdom

Latin American group: 20 members — Argentina, Bolivia, Brazil, Chile, Colombia, Costa Rica, Cuba, Dominican Republic, Ecuador, El Salvador, Guatemala, Haiti, Honduras, Mexico, Nicaragua, Panama, Paraguay, Peru, Uruguay, and Venezuela

Scandinavian group: 4 members — Denmark, Iceland, Norway, and Sweden

Western European group: 5 members — Belgium, France, Italy, Luxembourg, and the Netherlands

The newly organized African group began operating within the framework of the Thirteenth Session. The Scandinavian group might be placed in a separate category since, although it holds meetings, these meetings are generally held before the Assembly comes into session and not as often during the sessions as are those of the other caucusing groups. It is apparent that there is an overlapping of membership between the Asian-African, Arab, African, and Commonwealth groups, and between the Benelux and Western European groups.

The caucusing groups are the main political-interest groups that operate in the Assembly and are involved in behind-the-scene negotiations on most of the crucial issues. Ten members of the Assembly — Finland, Yugoslavia, China, Austria, Greece, Ireland, Portugal, Spain, Israel, and the United States — do not belong to any caucusing group.

GEOGRAPHICAL DISTRIBUTION GROUPS

Geographical distribution groups exist by virtue of informal "gentleman's agreements," consensus, or formal agreements [8] for the purpose of allocating seats on the General Committee, the three councils, the International Court of Justice, and other less-than-full membership committees.

[8] The only formal agreement is contained in General Assembly Res. 1192 (XII).

The term "geographical distribution" as applied to this category of political factions is really a misnomer. They are the result of a working political interpretation developed from the phraseology of Article 23 of the Charter, and any true geographical distribution in the groups is coincidental. They are generally referred to as geographical distribution groups because diplomatic tact prevents them from being called, more rationally, political compromise groups with some reflection of geographical areas. In essence, they consult only to agree upon which of their members are to be "nominated" so as to give a geographical distribution to the composition of the smaller bodies in the United Nations in accord with the number of seats allocated to the particular group.

There are five distinct geographical groups in which there is no overlap of membership:

Eastern European groups: 10 members — Albania, Bulgaria, Byelorussia, Czechoslovakia, Finland, Hungary, Poland, Rumania, Ukraine, and Yugoslavia

Asian and African group: 29 members — Afghanistan, Burma, Cambodia, Ceylon, Ethiopia, Ghana, Guinea, India, Indonesia, Iran, Iraq, Japan, Jordan, Laos, Lebanon, Liberia, Libya, Malaya, Morocco, Nepal, Pakistan, Philippines, Saudi Arabia, Sudan, Thailand, Tunisia, Turkey, United Arab Republic (Egypt and Syria), and Yemen

Latin American group: 20 members — Argentina, Bolivia, Brazil, Chile, Colombia, Costa Rica, Cuba, Dominican Republic, Ecuador, El Salvador, Guatemala, Haiti, Honduras, Mexico, Nicaragua, Panama, Paraguay, Peru, Uruguay, and Venezuela

Western European and other states group: 18 members — Australia, Austria, Belgium, Canada, Denmark, Greece, Iceland, Ireland, Israel, Italy, Luxembourg, the Netherlands, New Zealand, Norway, Portugal, Spain, Sweden, and the Union of South Africa

Permanent members of the Security Council group: 5 members — China, France, the Soviet Union, the United Kingdom, and the United States

In addition to these five geographical distribution groups, which are exclusive in membership, there is one other which has widely overlapping membership but which is also acknowledged in the distribution of elective seats,

Commonwealth group: 9 members — Australia, Canada, Ceylon, Ghana, India, Malaya, New Zealand, Pakistan, and the Union of South Africa

The members of the Commonwealth geographical distribution group are also either members of the Asian and African geographical distribution group or the Western European and Other States geographical distribution groups. Most of the election voting "agreements" provide that at least one of the members elected should be from the Commonwealth. Whichever Commonwealth member seat is secured will also count as a seat for the other geographical distribution group to which that Commonwealth member belongs.

It is fairly apparent from a glance at the memberships of the geographical distribution groups and the caucusing groups that these are in several instances identical groupings of states, and that in the other groupings there is considerable similarity of membership. Chart 1 which shows the interrelations of membership between these two general categories of interest groups in the General Assembly,[9] demonstrates the reason for much of the confusion about blocs and groups. It shows that the Soviet bloc and the Eastern European group are not identical in membership. It should also be noted that, although the Soviet Union is not actually a member of the Eastern European group from which the geographical distribution seats are chosen, the Soviet Union does participate in the meetings of the group to agree upon the group's candidates for an election. This situation is also true of the United Kingdom in the case of the Commonwealth geographical distribution group and of France in the Western European geographical distribution group.

Chart 1 also illustrates the fact the "geographical" distribution

[9] Acknowledgement must be given to David Blickenstaff (Director of The Paris Information Center, External Relations Division, UN Office of Public Information), who in 1952 (when he was a member of the Executive Office of the Secretary-General) first gave the author the idea of compiling this bloc list chart. The way in which these bloc list charts have developed since the initial idea is entirely the responsibility of the author.

groups do not represent true geographical divisions of states but are essentially efforts to arrive at a working division of major political interest subdivisions in the General Assembly. Any truly geographical division would: include China, the Union of South Africa, and Israel in the Asian and African Group instead of putting them elsewhere; somehow include Canada and the United States with the other Western Hemisphere states; include Austria with Eastern Europe; possibly include Greece with Eastern Europe. (Actually, in earlier sessions, Greece was given an "Eastern European" seat over the united protests of the other Eastern European Members.) Finland might just as well be with the other Scandinavian states in Western Europe as in Eastern Europe; and Australia and New Zealand might be in a separate category or with the Asian and African states. If geographical distribution were actually on a basis of geography, logic might make it much more appropriate to separate the African states from the Asian states. A more truly geographical division might be along the lines of the formula established in Article VI of the International Atomic Energy Agency Statute.

A. The Board of Governors shall be composed as follows:

1. The outgoing Board of Governors (or in the case of the first Board, the Preparatory Commission referred to in Annex I) shall designate for membership on the Board the five members most advanced in technology of atomic energy including the production of source materials and the member most advanced in the technology of atomic energy including the production of source materials in each of the following areas not represented by the aforesaid five:

    (1) North America
    (2) Latin America
    (3) Western Europe
    (4) Eastern Europe
    (5) Africa and Middle East
    (6) South Asia
    (7) South East Asia and the Pacific
    (8) Far East

2. The outgoing Board of Governors (or in the case of the first Board, the Preparatory Commission referred to in Annex I) shall designate for

membership on the Board two members from among the following other producers of source materials: Belgium, Czechoslovakia, Poland, and Portugal; and shall also designate for membership on the Board one other member as a supplier of technical assistance. No member in this category in any one year will be eligible for redesignation in the same category for the following year.

3. The General Conference shall elect ten members of membership on the Board of Governors, with due regard to equitable representation on the Board as a whole of the members in the areas listed in subparagraph A–1 of this article, so that the Board shall at all times include in this category a representative of each of those areas except North Africa. Except for the five members chosen for a term of one year in accordance with paragraph D of this article, no member in this category in any one term of office will be eligible for re-election in the same category for the following term of office.

B. The designations provided for in subparagraphs A–1 and A–2 of this article shall take place not less than sixty days before each regular annual session of the General Conference. The elections provided for in subparagraph A–3 of this article shall take place at regular annual sessions of the General Conference.

C. Members represented on the Board of Governors in accordance with subparagraphs A–1 and A–2 of this article shall hold office from the end of the next regular annual session of the General Conference after their designation until the end of the following regular annual session of the General Conference.

D. Members represented on the Board of Governors in accordance with subparagraph A–3 of this article shall hold office from the end of the regular annual session of the General Conference at which they are elected until the end of the second regular annual session of the General Conference thereafter. In the election of these members for the first Board, however, five shall be chosen for a term of one year.

The use of such a geographical formula as in the International Atomic Energy Agency depends upon a desire to elect upon a basis of actual geography rather than on a basis of political alliance. In an organ with a majority voting requirement like the General Assembly, the division into "geographical regions" can be determined on any criteria that satisfies the groups making up the majority, and the minority groups which are not united may find themselves "lumped together" in an wholly unrealistic "geographical region." The debate in the Special Political Committee in the XIIth Session of the Assembly, which finally resulted in the adoption of Resolution 1192 (XII) on the basis for the allocation of seats on the General Committee, reflected the dominant majority view that the geographical distribution groups, adhering to past practices and "informal agreements," represent a fairly identical correlation with the caucusing groups in the cases where the caucusing groups were with the majority groups passing the resolution.

As the Czechoslovakian delegate explained to the Special Political Committee:

Delegations had had two months in which to obtain all the necessary documents and to prepare themselves for the discussions. Moreover, for several weeks, some groups of countries had been holding preliminary talks on the way in which the problem could be solved. The draft resolution before the Committee was the result of those negotiations; countries of three geographical regions had agreed on a common position, whereas the objections came from the countries of one region only. . . .[10]

The three groups which he implied were supporting the resolution were the Soviet, Asian-African, and Latin American caucusing groups. He lumped all the other members as "one region — much to the consternation of these members. For example, France

pointed out that the group "Western Europe and other countries" in . . . the draft resolution bore no relation to facts. The European group, which did exist, had never held caucuses with the Commonwealth countries, the United States or any other countries. The expression "Western Europe and other countries" was an invention of the sponsors of the joint draft.[11]

That the geographical distribution groups are politically determined by the Assembly majority, rather than on any basis of actual geography was spelled out by the Czechoslovakian sponsor of this only formal distribution resolution, when he stated:

The specification of geographical regions was equally the result of informal negotiations among groups of countries. Those regions correspond

[10] UN Doc. A/SPC/SR. 81, 13 December 1957, p. 3.
[11] UN Doc. A/SPC/SR. 80, 11 December 1957, p. 17.

to the political realities which have been reflected for years in all United
Nations bodies. . . .[12]

In spite of the protests on the character of the geographical distribution groups, there is considerable correlation between them
and the caucusing groups, as indicated on Chart 1. Certainly any
efforts to alter the geographical distribution groups recognized by
the majority of the United Nations must recognize that those who
disagree with the present formal and informal agreements need to
alter the present caucusing group coalitions if they are to build a
majority supporting some other basis of geographical distribution
groups. Such action, therefore, would have to be directed either to
forming new caucusing groups or to winning over other caucusing
groups so as to build the necessary majority.

Chart 1 also indicates that, by virtue of membership in several
of the groups, some states possess pivotal positions making them
key states from the standpoint of political tactics. For example, the
fact that the United Arab Republic and Libya belong to the Arab,
African, and Asian-African groups means that they are members
which if cultivated by interested parties would offer access to at
least three fairly large caucusing groups. Similarly, Ghana as a
member of the African, Asian-African, and Commonwealth caucusing groups, is also in a key position. To a lesser degree, this is also
true of Ceylon, India, Malaya, and Pakistan, which belong to both
the Commonwealth and Asian-African caucusing groups.

REGIONAL GROUPS

Regional groups. In addition to the one bloc, eight caucusing
groups, and six geographical distribution groups which provide a
basis for group coalitions, there are two other categories of groupings which are factors in the political situation in the general Assembly. These might be termed *regional groups* and *common interest groups.* They are primarily distinguished by the fact that for
the most part they do not have any regular procedural or organizational features operating behind the scenes of the General Assembly

[12] UN Doc. A/SPC/SR. 81, 13 December 1957, p. 3.

but are groups of states bound together by certain factors present and operating independently of the framework of the United Nations.

The *regional groups* which might be distinguished are groups of UN members "bound" together either by common membership in a regional organization not connected directly with the United Nations, such as regional collective-security organizations, regional alliances, or regional economic organizations, or by common participation in important regional conferences which, while not establishing any permanent organization, nevertheless draw the participating countries together in establishing an agreement on principles of mutual consultation.

None of these regional groups caucuses in the General Assembly. However, since regional cooperation yields mutual agreement on certain areas of concern, there is good probability that such agreement is carried over into the General Assembly. This is certainly true if the regional agreements take the form of binding commitments. Although even in the case of binding commitments the issues reflected in the Assembly may not be precisely the same, it has been implied that these groups operate as a caucus in the Assembly, a point which is often denied. Following such implications, Mr. Lloyd of the United Kingdom explained to the Assembly that,

Mr. Gromyko (USSR) referred to them as "blocs." The countries of NATO do not vote as a bloc in this Assembly. We do not even hold meetings to discuss Assembly matters together, and we rarely, all of us, vote the same way. Exactly the same applies to the countries in the Baghdad Pact and the countries of SEATO. . . .[13]

The degree to which any regional organization, arrangement, or conference has a behind-the-scenes influence on the group politics of the General Assembly is difficult to determine because the specific concerns of the regional interest may bear on only one aspect of the Assembly's areas of concern. For example, such regional arrangements as the Baghdad Pact, the North Atlantic Treaty Organization, and the Southeast Asia Treaty Organization, which are to a great

[13] UN.GA.XII. *OR. Plenary*, 685th mtg., 24 September 1957, p. 98.

part concerned with collective defense against the Soviet Union, may have an influence primarily in the area of issues before the General Assembly which are concerned with aspects of East-West tension. Similarly, it might be argued that a regional arrangement like the Colombo Plan, concerned with uniting efforts for economic development, might reflect this joint concern in Assembly debates concerned with economic development. Certainly, one of the easiest ways of determining the possible effect of a regional arrangement in the Assembly is to examine the voting records of the regional arrangement members. If they evidence a greater degree of cohesion in the General Assembly after the conclusion of the regional "agreement" than before the "agreement," it may be a good indication that the regional arrangement operates as a group in the General Assembly — even though it may not hold any caucus meetings or consultations during the session.

For the purposes of this study 21 possible regional groups will be examined for evidence of cohesive voting in the Assembly. These might be termed the more "important" regional arrangements since they are the ones most often encountered in "corridor conversations" with members of delegations in the General Assembly. The twenty-one regional groups are: [14]

Anzus Council: 3 members — Australia, New Zealand, and the United States

Arab League: 10 members — Iraq, Jordan, Lebanon, Libya, Morocco, Saudi Arabia, Sudan, Tunisia, United Arab Republic (Egypt-Syria), and Yemen

Baghdad Pact: 5 members — Iraq, Iran, Pakistan, Turkey, and the United Kingdom

Balkan Alliance: 3 members — Greece, Turkey, and Yugoslavia

Bandung Conference: 25 members — Afghanistan, Burma, Cambodia, Ceylon, Ethiopia, Ghana, India, Indonesia, Iran, Iraq, Japan, Jordan, Laos, Lebanon, Liberia, Libya, Nepal, Pakistan, Philippines, Saudi Arabia,

[14] The number of members listed in each group include only those members of the group who are also members of the United Nations.

Sudan, Thailand, Turkey, United Arab Republic (Egypt-Syria), and Yemen

Colombo Plan: 17 members — Australia, Burma, Cambodia, Canada, Ceylon, India, Indonesia, Japan, Laos, Malaya, Nepal, New Zealand, Pakistan, Philippines, Thailand, United Kingdom, and the United States

Commonwealth: 9 members — Australia, Canada, Ceylon, Ghana, India, Malaya, New Zealand, Pakistan, and the Union of South Africa

Conference of Independent African States: 8 members — Ethiopia, Ghana, Liberia, Libya, Morocco, Sudan, Tunisia, and the United Arab Republic

Council of Europe: 14 members — Austria, Belgium, Denmark, France, Greece, Iceland, Ireland, Italy, Luxembourg, the Netherlands, Norway, Sweden, Turkey, and the United Kingdom

European Atomic Energy Community: 5 members — Belgium, France, Italy, Luxembourg, and the Netherlands

European Coal and Steel Community: 5 members — Belgium, France, Italy, Luxembourg, and the Netherlands

European Common Market: 5 members — Belgium, France, Italy, Luxembourg, and the Netherlands

European Payments Union: 15 members — Austria, Belgium, Denmark, France, Greece, Iceland, Ireland, Italy, the Netherlands, Luxembourg, Norway, Portugal, Sweden, Turkey, and the United Kingdom

Nordic Council: 4 members — Denmark, Iceland, Norway, and Sweden

North Atlantic Treaty Organization: 14 members — Belgium, Canada, Denmark, France, Greece, Iceland, Italy, Luxembourg, the Netherlands, Norway, Portugal, Turkey, United Kingdom, and the United States

Organization for European Economic Cooperation: 15 members — Austria, Belgium, Denmark, France, Greece, Iceland, Ireland, Italy, Luxembourg, the Netherlands, Norway, Portugal, Sweden, Turkey, and the United Kingdom

Organization of American States: 21 members — Argentina, Bolivia, Brazil, Chile, Colombia, Costa Rica, Cuba, Dominican Republic, Ecuador, El Salvador, Guatemala, Haiti, Honduras, Mexico, Nicaragua, Panama, Paraguay, Peru, Uruguay, Venezuela, and the United States

Organization of Central American States: 5 members — Costa Rica, El Salvador, Guatemala, Honduras, and Nicaragua

South East Asia Treaty Organization: 8 members — Australia, France, New Zealand, Pakistan, Philippines, Thailand, United Kingdom and the United States

Warsaw Pact: 7 members — Albania, Bulgaria, Czechoslovokia, Hungary, Poland, Rumania, and the Soviet Union

Western European Union: 6 members — Belgium, France, Italy, Luxembourg, the Netherlands, and the United Kingdom

A glance at the membership of these regional groups makes it apparent that there is a great deal of similarity, if not identity, between the regional groups and the caucusing groups, and that in most instances there is also a considerable overlap of membership between the various regional groups.

Probably the best way to make evident the extent of similarity and overlap of membership between the regional groups themselves and the caucusing groups is to examine them region by region. Chart 2 compares the "Western European" countries as to their membership in various regional groups with the caucusing groups. Several points become fairly obvious. The memberships of the Western European caucusing group, the European Atomic Energy Community, the European Common Market, and the European Coal and Steel Community are identical. The memberships of the Nordic Council and the Scandinavian caucusing group are also identical. The Benelux caucusing group is identical with the Benelux Customs Union. Although this latter regional body was not listed as a regional group, it might well have been included. The high degree of overlapping membership between the other "Western European" regional groups indicates that, although they may not be identical with any caucusing groups, nonetheless these countries have, through their membership in these regional bodies, many elements of common interest. Further, all of the members of these "Western European" regional groups are also members of the Western European geographical distribution group.

Chart 3 illustrates the overlapping memberships between the "Asian and African" regional groups and caucusing groups. The African caucusing group is identical to the Conference of African

States, the Arab League is identical to the Arab caucusing group, and all of the members of the Bandung Conference are members of the Asian-African caucusing group. If the Commonwealth were included in this list of regional groups, it would be apparent that its membership is identical with that of the Commonwealth caucusing group.

Chart 4 illustrates the membership in the "American" regional bodies in relationship to the Latin American caucusing group, and Chart 5 shows the "Eastern European" regional groups in relation to the membership of the Soviet caucusing group.

These four charts suggest that certain members are in rather key positions. Turkey is a member of the Asian-African caucusing group, the Baghdad Pact, and the North Atlantic Treaty Organization as well as the Council of Europe, the European Payments Union, and the Organization of European Economic Cooperation. Iraq is a member of both the Arab and Asian-African caucusing groups and of the Arab League, and the Bandung Conference. France, Belgium, Luxembourg, the Netherlands, and Italy as well as Norway, Denmark, and Iceland belong both to caucusing groups and to most of the European regional groups. Many other such pertinent relationships are obvious from a close study of these charts and suggest possible political roles for the members.

It should be pointed out that many of the regional groups have been formed for specific purposes and that their reflection of regional group consensus in the General Assembly is generally limited to the particular issues upon which they have developed common points of view. Their real importance might well be viewed as indicating certain common interests which might provide a basis for forming new caucusing groups as the General Assembly develops. Obviously, many of the regional groups may espouse concepts which are not wholly in accord with other regional groups and particularly with other regional groups that belong to the same caucusing groups. For example, there certainly are many divisive forces in the Asian-African caucusing group when it is made of such "conflicting" regional groups as the Arab League, the Baghdad Pact, and

SEATO, to give but one illustration. This fact will become even more apparent when these groups are considered individually.

COMMON INTEREST GROUPS

Common interest groups might be defined as groups of states which, although not bound together by any sort of formal arrangement or membership in a regional body, nevertheless have some elements in common which tend to provide a common outlook on certain types of issues before the General Assembly. Whether these common interest groups actually exist may be a moot question; some observers indicate that they do exist and have an influence. At least seven might be distinguished:

Moslem States: 15 members — Afghanistan, Indonesia, Iran, Iraq, Jordan, Lebanon, Libya, Morocco, Pakistan, Saudi Arabia, Sudan, Tunisia, Turkey, United Arab Republic (Egypt-Syria), and Yemen

Arab States: 10 members — Iraq, Jordan, Lebanon, Libya, Morocco, Saudi Arabia, Sudan, Tunisia, United Arab Republic (Egypt-Syria), and Yemen

Big Three: 3 members — France, United Kingdom, and the United States

Trust Administrators: 7 members — Australia, Belgium, France, Italy, New Zealand, United Kingdom, and the United States

Colonial Powers: [15] 10 members — Australia, Belgium, France, Italy, the Netherlands, New Zealand, Portugal, Spain, United Kingdom, and the United States

Anti-Colonial States: 37 members — Afghanistan, Albania, Bulgaria, Burma, Byelorussia, Cambodia, Ceylon, Czechoslovakia, Ethiopia, Ghana, Guinea, Hungary, India, Indonesia, Iran, Iraq, Jordan, Laos, Lebanon, Liberia, Libya, Malaya, Morocco, Nepal, Pakistan, Philippines, Poland, Rumania, Saudi Arabia, Sudan, Thailand, Tunisia, Ukraine, USSR, United Arab Republic, Yemen, and Yugoslavia

Underdeveloped Countries: 57 members — Afghanistan, Argentina, Austria, Bolivia, Brazil, Burma, Cambodia, Ceylon, Chile, China, Colom-

[15] "Colonial" and "anti-colonial" are terms used in referring to these groups of members and in no way imply an application of the actual definition of these terms.

bia, Costa Rica, Cuba, Dominican Republic, Ecuador, El Salvador, Ethiopia, Finland, Ghana, Greece, Guatamala, Guinea, Haiti, Honduras, Iceland, India, Indonesia, Iran, Iraq, Israel, Japan, Jordan, Laos, Lebanon, Liberia, Libya, Malaya, Mexico, Morocco, Nepal, Nicaragua, Pakistan, Panama, Paraguay, Peru, Philippines, Saudi Arabia, Spain, Sudan, Thailand, Tunisia, Turkey, United Arab Republic, Uruguay, Venezuela, Yemen, and Yugoslavia

These groupings are not derived from abstract reasoning but are based on discussion with members of delegations. There is considerable correlation between the membership in these common interest groups and the caucusing groups, as is shown in Chart 6. In essence, the so-called anti-colonial states as a group consists of the Soviet and Asian-African caucusing groups, excluding Japan and Turkey. Logic might exclude Austria and Finland from the "underdeveloped countries," but most individuals consulted indicated that they are generally included in this common interest group. These groups do not, of course, have any formal organization, but they have obvious common ties which doubtless provide a sense of cohesion in particular issues. Chart 6 indicates that for the most part they are actually either coalitions of caucusing groups or coalitions of the majority of members from the various caucusing groups.

TEMPORARY GROUPS

There seem to have been at least three temporary groups which have materialized on particular issues before the Assembly in certain sessions:

Spanish Language group: The Spanish speaking countries of Latin America plus the Philippines, which exerted an influence in several sessions on questions pertaining to Spanish language documents and Spanish as a working language of the United Nations

The Sixteen: The sixteen members of the United Nations, that sent combat troops to Korea, and seem to have maintained regular consultations with respect to matters of joint concern

South East Asian Prime Ministers: India, Indonesia, Ceylon, and Pakistan have held meetings outside the United Nations which have been reflected in the Assembly, especially in the Suez situation in 1956

Other temporary groups may well have existed since it is only natural that special consultations or coalitions are worked out on certain specific issues in certain sessions; but it would be difficult if not impossible to determine all the special temporary groupings that have developed on particular issues before the United Nations.

The bloc and group patterns in the United Nations have been a gradual but steady development. Some of the caucusing groups, such as the Latin American, Commonwealth, and Arab groups, were in existence at the San Francisco Conference; others have gradually emerged. The geographical distribution groups have been in existence in one form or another since the First Part of the First Session. The regional groups have emerged as particular regional organizations have come into being over the twelve-year history of the organization. The common interest groups have been inherent in the Assembly from the outset. The growth of the bloc and group pattern is to a considerable extent a reflection of the expanding membership of the organization. As the United Nations has grown in size, like interests, cohesive factors, and joint participation in other international organizations have drawn members into group relations in order to have a more effective vote bargaining power.

Any understanding of the development and significance of blocs and groups in the Assembly has to start with an examination of them individually. When did they come into existence? Who has belonged to the group? How has the group membership been increased or altered? What are the cohesive and divisive elements evident in each group? How has the formation of the group been reflected in voting in the Assembly? These are the sorts of questions that this part of the study will attempt to answer. The real test of the impact of the formation of groups is in the effect it has had on the Assembly; the effect it has had in unifying the efforts of the members of the group, and the effect it has had in votes of the group in relation to other members of the Assembly. Because voting — bloc voting — provides a real test of the effect of the group actions, stress is placed on examining the voting record of the group. It is only after the groups have been examined in such detail that it is possible to see the interrelations of the groups on the development of the General Assembly.

THE SOVIET CAUCUSING BLOC

The Soviet bloc is the most tightly organized and cohesive interest group in the Assembly, making itself constantly felt not only through almost identical voting but also through coordinated tactics in the presentation of the bloc's positions in the procedural and substantive discussions in the plenary and the main committees.

The nucleus of the Soviet bloc was provided when the San Francisco Conference admitted Byelorussia and the Ukraine as original members of the United Nations organization. Byelorussia, the Ukraine, and the Soviet Union combined with Yugoslavia and Poland initially as a caucusing group. They became a bloc where the Soviet Union extended its complete influence over Poland and the Cominform was constituted in 1947 to coordinate and central-ize the political role of the satellites. The bloc was enlarged follow-ing the coup in Czechoslovakia in February 1948 and became more solidified as a result of the Molotov Plan in January 1949, which completed the economic integration of the satellites. Yugoslavia, initially an integral member, broke with the Cominform in 1948, leaving the bloc with a core membership of five until the admission of Albania, Bulgaria, Hungary, and Rumania in December 1955 in-creased it to nine. Thus the membership history is as follows:

General Assembly Sessions I through II — 1946 to June 1948

(5)	Byelorussia	Ukraine	Yugoslavia
	Poland	USSR	

General Assembly Sessions III through X — June 1948 to December 1955

(5)	Byelorussia	Poland	USSR
	Czechoslovakia	Ukraine	

General Assembly Session XI to the present — 1956 to 1958

(9)	Albania	Czechoslovakia	Rumania
	Bulgaria	Hungary	Ukraine
	Byelorussia	Poland	USSR

Meetings of the Soviet bloc, which are held in delegation offices regularly during the Assembly sessions and reportedly presided over by the ranking Soviet delegate, apparently result in "decisions" which are binding on the members. Moreover, it seems clear that it is the political, military, and economic domination of the Soviet Union over the other members of the bloc which ensures that the group speak with one voice. As long as Soviet dominance is main-tained, there seems little likelihood that the bloc will operate on any basis short of Soviet direction.

One has to infer the degree of inner cohesion in the Soviet bloc. Until their complete domination by the Soviet Union, Poland and Czechoslovakia displayed a minor sort of independent action. Some observers have felt that the implications of Titoism may extend to the other satellites. The shifting of political forces within the Soviet

Union since the death of Stalin has resulted in ideological shifts which may in part explain both the Polish move for a greater autonomy and the Hungarian revolt in November 1956. Whether such pressures will continue and manifest themselves in the bloc's actions in the United Nations is impossible to say. No such tendency has been evidenced in the period from 1956 to 1959.

An examination of the voting record of the Soviet bloc in the General Assembly, using an adjusted gross [1] of the roll-call votes in the plenary and the main committees as a basis of analysis, makes certain facts apparent. Through the XIIIth Session the Soviet bloc [2] has been divided [3] only once (0.2 per cent) on the vote in the IInd Session on a Danish amendment to a resolution on South West Africa (Res. 141–II). This Danish amendment urged that the Union of South Africa propose a trust agreement on South West Africa as soon as possible. Poland voted "no"; Yugoslavia, the Soviet Union, and the Ukraine voted "yes"; Byelorussia abstained. But there seems to have been no real difference of opinion in the bloc on the issue, and the divided vote is generally regarded as a question of "mixed signals," explained by the nature of the procedure of voting in the Assembly. On roll-call votes the name of a member of the Assembly is drawn from a "fishbowl" and the voting begins with that member followed by the others in alphabetical order. In most cases, therefore, the Soviet Union is not the first member of the Soviet bloc to cast its vote; and if all members of the bloc are not clear as to how they should vote, there is the possibility that they may cast a "wrong" vote. There have been several occasions when one of the Soviet bloc members, voting before the Soviet Union, has abstained and then requested the right to change its vote after it became aware that it was not voting as it "should." [4]

[1] The *adjusted gross* is explained on page 20.

[2] The membership of the bloc is the membership that has actually existed in the various sessions as detailed above.

[3] Divided: when some of the bloc members voted "yes", others "no" and in some instances other members may abstain.

[4] As a general procedure members are not allowed to change a vote once it has been cast.

In addition to the one divided vote, the bloc has cast 20 solidarity votes [5] (3.84 per cent of the adjusted gross). These have involved:

(1) Consultative arrangements of nongovernmental organizations with the Economic and Social Council (Res. 49C-1). Soviet Union and Yugoslavia abstained, with the rest of the bloc voting "no."

(2) Regional conferences of non-self-governing territories' peoples (Res. 67-I). Poland "yes," rest abstained.

(3) Trusteeship agreements for French Cameroons and French Togoland (Res. 63-I), 2 votes. Poland abstained, rest "no."

(4) Draft resolution on Temporary Administration of Jerusalem (4 votes in second special session). In one of these votes Poland abstained while the rest voted "no"; in another Byelorussia voted "no" and the others abstained; and in the other two votes Yugoslavia voted "no" while the other abstained.

(5) Reports of the Atomic Energy Commission (2 votes on a defeated Indian amendment to Resolution 191-III). Czechoslovakia abstained while the rest voted "no."

(6) Observation of human rights in Hungary and Bulgaria (preamble of Res. 272-III). Yugoslavia and Ukraine voted "yes," rest abstained.

(7) Attempt to overrule President's ruling on Polish request to include item of Gerhart Eisler on the Third Session agenda. Ukraine voted "yes," Czechoslovakia abstained, the rest did not participate in the vote.

(8) Credentials of representatives (par. 1 of Res. 609A-VII) approving the first report of the Credentials Committee. Poland and the Ukraine abstained, the rest voted "no." The second paragraph of this resolution postponed considerations on the credentials of the Republic of China.

(9) Hungarian situation in the second emergency special session (3 votes — on a South African amendment to Res. 1005-ESS-II). Poland abstained while the rest voted "no." On a joint amendment to delete reference to USSR interference with food and refugees to Res. ESS-II

[5] For convenience, votes in which one or several members of a bloc or group "abstain" while all the others vote one way (i.e., either "yes" or "no") are referred to as "solidarity" votes. That is, the members of the bloc did not vote against each other although some members may have abstained. These votes are called solidarity votes because the implication of this type of voting is that while some members of a group or bloc may disagree with the other members they "abstain" rather than vote against the other members of the bloc or group.

and on Resolution 1007 on assistance to the Hungarian people, Hungary and Poland voted "yes" while the rest of the bloc abstained.

(10) Hungarian situation in the XIth Session (2 votes — on Res. 1128-XI, re observers be admitted "without prejudice to its sovereignty." Albania, Bulgaria, Ukraine, and the USSR voted "yes," while the rest abstained. On Res. 1129-XI calling for aid to refugees, Hungary and Rumania voted "no" while the others abstained.

(11) Expansion of international trade (Res. 1156-XII), operative paragraph urging approval of Organization for Trade Cooperation. Czechoslovakia abstained while the rest voted "no."

(12) Promotion of the international flow of private capital to less developed countries (Res. 1318-XIII). Byelorussia abstained while the rest voted "no."

The divergences in many of these instances might be attributed to "mixed signals" (i.e., items 1, 4, 5, 6, 7, 8, 11, and 12). The early votes of Poland (i.e., items 2 and 3) might be the result of the fact that Poland at the time of these votes was not wholly dominated by the Soviet Union. Some United Nations observers, however, feel that the differences in the votes on the Hungarian situation (i.e., items 9 and 10) may have been "independent" decisions of the Polish and Hungarian delegations. Even so, this list indicates that the solidarity votes hardly represent divisions within the Soviet bloc.

No other interest faction has a record of identical voting such as that manifested by the Soviet bloc. In 95.97 per cent of the adjusted gross roll-call votes members of the Soviet bloc voted identically.[6] Chart 7, showing the types of votes (i.e., identical, solidarity, or divided) of the Soviet bloc session by session, is not in itself all-important, but it is of considerable interest when compared with similar charts on the other caucusing groups present in the Assembly.

An interesting question is whether this high degree of voting cohesion is used effectively by the bloc to ally itself with the posi-

[6] Identical: All members voted the same; none abstained unless they all abstained.

tion of the majority of the General Assembly. Several trends seem evident in analyzing the relationship of the voting of the Soviet bloc to the voting of the majority of the Assembly. Chart 8 shows both the percentage by which the bloc is "in agreement" with the majority of the General Assembly [7] and the percentage by which it is "not against" the majority of the Assembly.[8] It can be argued that the total of the votes of the bloc "in agreement" and "not against" represents the maximum number of votes in which the bloc finds itself in agreement with the majority of the Members of the General Assembly.

Chart 8 indicates that the Soviet bloc is "in agreement" with the majority of the General Assembly on the average between 30 per cent and 60 per cent of the time. On a total adjusted gross base it is in the Assembly majority 39.4 per cent of the time. Chart 8 suggests that up to the Xth Session there was a tendency to increase the degree of abstentions rather than to oppose the Assembly majority. Whether this was an intentional trend or not is difficult to ascertain. The fluctuations session by session are explained to a large degree by the character of the votes that dominated the regular sessions. Analyzing the subject of the votes [9] reveals that the regular sessions

[7] "In agreement" with the majority means that all or a majority of a bloc or group voted identically with the majority of the General Assembly necessary to pass or defeat an issue.

[8] Solidarity or "not against" the majority, means that all or a majority of a bloc or group abstained rather than voting either with or against the majority of the General Assembly which passed or defeated an issue. Admittedly, abstentions might contribute to the defeat of an issue, especially in the cases where a two-thirds majority is required, because of the failure to support. However, because Rule 88 (127) of the General Assembly Rules of Procedure (Doc. A/3660, 6 September 1957) provides that "Members which abstain from voting are not considered as voting" and decisions are made by a majority of the Members "present and voting" (Rules 85, 86, 87 [126]) it can be argued that members who abstain are not of sufficient conviction to vote either with or against the majority, and, therefore, are actually neuter — "not against." At least, this is the criteria that has been applied in this monograph, and if it is in error, it is an error equally applied throughout the analysis and qualifications can be made accordingly.

[9] The subject-of-votes categories of analysis are explained on page 24.

in which the Soviet bloc was in the largest percentage of agreement were those in which the largest percentage of the votes was concerned with issues involving self-determination or administrative-procedural-structural matters. The bloc was in accord with the Assembly majority to the highest degree in the Fourth, Sixth, Eighth, and Tenth Regular Sessions. Records show that 47.8 per cent of the votes in the Fourth Session, 34.8 per cent of the votes in the Sixth Session, and 36.3 per cent of the votes in the Eighth Session were concerned with self-determination issues.[10] Of the votes in the Tenth Session, 72.3 per cent were on issues that are essentially administrative-procedural-structural matters. On the basis of these figures it might be inferred that when the majority of issues involve matters that can be categorized as self-determination or administrative-procedural-structural in nature the Soviet bloc is in greatest agreement with the majority of the Members of the General Assembly.

An examination of the subject and type of the votes in which the Soviet bloc was "in agreement" with the Assembly majority and of the votes in which the bloc abstained (i.e., "not against") instead of either supporting or opposing the Assembly majority probably provides a more accurate indication of the areas in which the bloc is effective in a parliamentary sense. Classifying the votes as to their subject matter, Chart 9 indicates the over-all percentage of the votes in which the Soviet bloc is "in agreement" — that is, supporting the position of the majority of the General Assembly. This chart indicates that the bloc is with the Assembly majority on 54.4 per cent of the human rights issues, 44.6 per cent of the self-determination issues, 41.0 per cent of the administrative, procedural, and structural issues, 39.4 per cent of the peaceful settlement issues, 38.0 per cent of the development of international law issues, 32.5 per cent of the economic, social, and humanitarian cooperation issues, and only 15.9 per cent of the collective measures and such issues as the regulation of armaments. Classifying these same issues as to the

[10] Unless otherwise indicated, these and the following figures are based on an adjusted gross number of roll-call votes.

type of action [11] required by the vote, Chart 10 indicates that the bloc is with the majority of the General Assembly in 41.2 per cent of the votes requiring states to take some direct action, 63.5 per cent of the votes requiring states to supply funds or information, and 36.3 per cent of the votes calling for some other type of action which does not involve states directly.

In view of the slight trend up to the Xth Session for more abstentions by the Soviet bloc, it is pertinent to note the kind of issues on which the bloc abstains. Chart 11 indicates that the bloc has abstained most often on collective measure and regulation of armaments issues (i.e., 15.7 per cent). On most of the other subjects it has abstained 11 per cent or less. Chart 12 indicates the abstentions of the bloc according to the type of implementation recommended in the votes. Here it has abstained most on issues recommending direct action by states (13.4 per cent) and least on actions recommending implementation other than by states (6.6 per cent).

Some interesting conclusions are suggested by the voting record of the Soviet bloc. In the first place, it would appear that it is perhaps the only true bloc in the sense that the members vote identically almost all of the time; and the record offers little indication that in the foreseeable future it will operate as anything but a bloc with nine identical votes (its present voting strength).

It follows that the bloc gives the Soviet Union in effect a multiple vote. More than that, although it operates in the Assembly as a unit, the bloc's several voices make possible a repetition of speeches, a propaganda technique which is sometimes rather successful. On the other hand, from the point of view of give-and-take negotiations with other states, the Soviet bloc has not the flexibility of the other

---

[11] The basis of the type-of-action categories of analysis are explained on pages 24–26. In essence, it is suggested that there are the kind or types, of recommendations varying as to the degree of "obligation," from a request that a state act (i.e. withdraw troops, etc.), to a request that a state help the organization (by supplying information or funds), to a request that a state do nothing but a request for action by some part of the organization (a committee, a council, the Secretary-General, etc.).

caucusing groups. Under the "guidance" of the Soviet Union it takes rigid positions which prevent it from making the kind of adjustments that are necessary if a bloc is to be successful in "riding" with the majority of the General Assembly most of the time.

In the context of united but inflexible action, the inferences to be drawn as to attitudes toward United Nations' issues take on considerable meaning when we note what does and what does not enlist Soviet bloc support.

The bloc is more willing to support issues concerned with human rights than any other — in other words, issues which so far in the history of the United Nations do not involve any recommended implementation by states except possibly to supply some information. The bloc may support a good many of the self-determination and peaceful settlement proposals — proposals which most often recommend implementation by states that are not members of the bloc. In fact, where the bloc disagrees with the majority on self-determination it is because the proposals are not forceful enough in their recommendations. The bloc tends to support proposals which are concerned with administrative, procedural, or structural matters — few of which involve any recommended actions; and it is with the majority on 64.3 per cent of the votes requiring states to supply funds or information, most of which involve show-of-hands rather than roll-call votes. By contrast, the Soviet bloc is most seldom with the majority of the United Nations on collective measures and such issues as the regulation of armaments — the fundamental issues concerned with the maintenance of peace and security. There it has been generally in opposition to the majority will of the General Assembly.

In sum, it would seem that the Soviet bloc, in supporting issues requiring little or no bloc commitment while opposing fundamental collective security measures, not only is in opposition to the majority in the United Nations on vital general concerns but also, by that very fact, in the minority on most of the issues vitally affecting Soviet political and strategic interests.

THE ARAB CAUCUSING GROUP

The Arab caucusing group has been operating as an interest group ever since the San Francisco Conference and is therefore one of the few such groups that has been in existence during the entire course of the history of the General Assembly. Its organizational nucleus was the Pact of the League of Arab States which was signed at a conference in Cairo on March 22, 1945, by Egypt, Iraq, Lebanon, Saudi Arabia, Syria, Trans-Jordan (now Jordan), and Yemen. The Arab League was joined by Libya in 1953 and the Sudan in 1956, when those states became independent and by Morocco and Tunisia in October 1958. Although the Arab League is the basis of the Arab group in the General Assembly, the caucusing group has included the members of the Arab League only as they have become members of the United Nations. Egypt, Iraq, Lebanon, Saudi Arabia, and Syria were original members of the United Nations in 1945; Yemen became a member in 1947, Jordan, Libya, Morocco and Tunisia in 1955, and Sudan in 1956. Because Morocco and Tunisia were not members of the Arab League when they were admitted to the United Nations — they were not immediately brought into the group on a regular basis.

The history of membership is as follows:

General Assembly Session I to II — 1946 to 29 September 1947
(5)	Egypt	Lebanon	Syria
	Iraq	Saudi Arabia	

General Assembly Sessions II through X —
30 September 1947 to 13 December 1955
(6)	Egypt	Lebanon	Syria
	Iraq	Saudi Arabia	Yemen

General Assembly 1st and 2nd Emergency Special Sessions —
14 December 1955 to 11 November 1956
(8)	Egypt	Lebanon	Syria
	Iraq	Libya	Yemen
	Jordan	Saudi Arabia	

General Assembly Sessions XI through XII —
12 November 1956 to 14 December 1957

(11)	Egypt	Libya	Sudan
	Iraq	Morocco	Tunisia
	Jordan	Saudi Arabia	Yemen
	Lebanon	Syria	

General Assembly 3rd Emergency Special Session to the present —
8 August 1958 to 1959

(10)	Iraq	Morocco	United Arab Republic
	Jordan	Saudi Arabia	Yemen
	Lebanon	Sudan	
	Libya	Tunisia	

The unification of Egypt and Syria into the United Arab Republic early in 1958, which included the unification of their foreign offices, reduced the voting membership of the Arab caucusing group from eleven to ten. The group does not include other Arab "states" which are not members of the United Nations, such as Algeria, Oman, Kuwait, and Mauritania. Should these areas become independent in the future and also new members, there is the possibility that they may become members of the group.

The caucusing group held meetings both on tactics and joint policies at the San Francisco Conference in 1945 and at that time submitted several joint proposals and amendments on matters of common concern. Since then it has not only met almost daily during the sessions of the General Assembly but also at intervals during the rest of the year to help coordinate policies pursued by Arab members elected to the Councils of the United Nations. It does not appear to concern itself with all issues before the Assembly but to concentrate on those related to the Middle East (i.e., re: Israel, refugees, Suez, economic development) and to the application of the principle of self-determination (i.e., Algeria, West Irian). The meetings of the group are secret and limited to the Heads of Delegations.

The group caucus also includes a representative from the Arab League who is accredited to the General Assembly as an observer and who apparently presides over caucus meetings. (The Arab League maintains an office in New York City in conjunction with the Arab Information Center and the Arab States Delegation Offices, which have a common United Nations Section.) In more recent sessions observers report that a representative from Oman (accredited to the United Nations as an Observer) has sat in on the meetings of the group. Representatives of Algerian National Liberation Front have participated in meetings of the group especially since September 1958 when they proclaimed a provisional government for the Algerian Republic. In a similar manner, the nationalist forces in Morocco and Tunisia met with the group earlier before they became independent and members of the United Nations. Although formal votes may be taken in the meetings, in which all caucus members have one vote, efforts are made to reach a consensus. Votes are not binding but imply a moral obligation. Moreover, preliminary negotiations generally indicate which issues are "noncontroversial," and there seems to be a real effort to keep the caucus from considering issues on which the members are divided.

In terms of regularity of meetings and planned tactics this group is one of the more active caucusing groups in the General Assembly. It acts both independently and as an organized unit within the Asian-African group. Several members of the Arab group are also members of the newly formed African caucusing group, and presumably the policies of the Arab groups will be pushed by those members in the African group meetings.

As a whole, the Arab caucusing group has been fairly effective in presenting a united front to the Assembly — much more so than most caucusing groups. In addition, it has used its "united front" effectively in working out alliances with other groups and consequently finds itself in the majority of the United Nations a good proportion of the time. Many observers feel that the seeming unity of this group is primarily due to its common opposition to Israel, and that the divisive elements inherent in the group have been minimized by the prolonged attention of the United Nations to the problem of Palestine. More recent events, such as the unification of Egypt and Syria and the abortive federation of Iraq and Jordan, have been pointed to as evidence of divisive forces inherent in the group which may become dominant if the unifying catalyst of Israel should lose the strong effect it has had in the past.

What, then, are some of the cohesive and divisive forces present in this group of states?

It can be argued, superficially at least, that there are many common factors which act to unify the members of the Arab caucusing group. It can be stressed that they have a common religion, common historical unity, common cultural heritage, and common language; that they face common problems of economic development and have comparable social structures; and that until recently all were European-dominated and have common feelings as a result of their newly won independence. These common factors appear compelling, and they do form a basis upon which to build Arab unity. The philosophy behind the League of Arab States itself was to establish an organization with "loose" ties and a "limited functional unity" as a goal, with "gradualism" as their method.[12] However, detailed examination suggests they are not as cohesive as they appear at first glance.

It is true that there has been a common historical unity, but the uniting factors were generally non-Arab Moslem elements. Historically, unity was generally imposed by military contact — not integration; and the weakness of the central ruling organ encouraged individual local developments and a pattern of political separateness.

In turn, although all of the Arab states lack modern economies, they are in different stages of economic development, and they do not complement each other economically. They have competing products; and all need primary raw materials like iron, wood, and coal, and lack investment capital and technical know-how — a situation which leads to competition instead of unity. Probably the nearest thing to economic unity was imposed during the Second World

[12] The Arab Information Center, *The Arab League, Its Origin — Purposes — Structure and Activities* (Information Paper 1, New York, 1955), pp. 9–10.

War in the form of the Middle East Supply Center. Similarly, there is no unity in the rate of social development, which ranges from that of Lebanon, with a developing middle class, to that of feudal Yemen and the nomadic societies constituting the bulk of Iraq, Jordan, and Saudi Arabia.

Although the Moslem religion and Arabic language do provide elements which can be used to instill a common sense of nationalism, the Arab area has been characterized by competing nationalist movements. (Of course, not all the states are Moslem; in Lebanon there is a small Christian majority.) The political systems in each of the states have considerable differences. Saudi Arabia and Yemen are theocratic monarchies; Jordan is a parliamentary monarchy with feudal oligarchy; Lebanon is a feudal oligarchy; and the United Arab Republic and Iraq have military dictatorships. Egypt, Syria, Morocco and Tunisia and Lebanon have a French base to their legal systems, Iraq and Jordan a British; Yemen and Saudi Arabia are primarily Moslem law states.

Thus the superficial view of natural Arab unity is somewhat misleading. There is, so to speak, a balance still to be struck between cohesive and divisive internal forces in the several Arab states; and to a large extent it has been external factors that have produced the appearance of unity among them and the capability for common action. We have only to note, for instance, the effects of the deep-rooted Arab opposition to the state of Israel and suspicion of the great powers that have supported Israel. In addition, there is a sense of united opposition to the so-called colonial powers because of the residual fears of domination, enhanced after the Suez intervention in 1956. But there is the obvious question of the permanence of such external influences. It would seem that the unity of the Arab caucusing group has tended to decrease as outside powers have stepped up their activities in the region, i.e., British and American sponsorship of the Baghdad Pact and the Soviet penetration in Egypt and Syria.

With the foregoing generalizations in mind, let us turn to an examination of the voting record for evidence of the degree of cohesiveness of the Arab caucusing group.

Chart 13 shows the degree to which the group has voted identically, the degree of solidarity (i.e., votes on which some members of the group abstained), and the extent to which the group has been divided. In the IIId Session, the group differed on issues involving several aspects of human rights; however rather than vote against each other they abstained, a fact that accounts for the lower percentage of identical voting in this session. Through the Xth Session of the Assembly the group was divided on 9.4 per cent of the votes. From then to the XIIIth Session it was divided on 17.8 per cent of the votes. A glance at the chart shows that there has also been a decline in identical voting by the group since the Xth Session. According to the votes, then, the solidarity of the Arab caucusing group would seem to have been loosening up.

An examination of the percentage of the votes in which individual members opposed the majority of the group gives a clue to the nature of the divisive trend beginning in the Xth Session. The votes of Morocco and Tunisia are not included in this particular examination because they joined the group so late. From the Ist Session through the IXth Session, individual members of the group were opposed to the majority of the group according to the following percentages:

Lebanon	2.32	Egypt	1.16	Iraq	0.86
Saudi Arabia	1.45	Yemen	0.96	Syria	0.86

From the Xth Session to the XIIIth the percentages were:

Iraq	10.6	Libya	2.78	Yemen	0.71
Lebanon	7.8	Saudi Arabia	0.71	Egypt	0.0
Jordan	3.7	Syria	0.71	Sudan	0.0

It would appear that Egypt in particular has been in control of the group since it has never been in opposition to the majority. At the same time, Iraq, which up to the Xth Session was in agreement with the group all but 0.86 per cent of the time, has been in opposition to the group 10.6 per cent of the time since the Xth Session. Admittedly, Iraq is still with the group on the vast majority of the votes, but, considered in the light of the past voting record, this change seems to be significant. A large part of the explanation of the shift of Iraq is probably to be found in the Baghdad Pact (signed in 1955 before the Xth Session of the Assembly), which created the Middle East Treaty Organization with Iraq, Turkey, Iran, Pakistan, and the United Kingdom. Since the Pact, of course, both the commitments of Iraq and the relationships of Iraq with Egypt have been altered, culminating in tensions between the United Arab Republic (Egypt and Syria) on one hand and the defunct Arab Federation of Iraq and Jordan on the other hand. Note should be made of the change in the voting of Lebanon since 1955, which indicates that Lebanon also has differed to a greater degree from the majority of the group than it did in the past.

In effect, then, the voting record suggests the existence of poles of opposition within the Arab group, but it also indicates that internal disagreement has had little real effect on the group voting pattern. Considering all the adjusted gross roll-call votes from the Ist Session through the XIIth Session, the group has voted identically 62.5 per cent of the time and has cast solidarity votes 27.7 per cent of the time. In other words, on 90.2 per cent of the votes the group has either voted identically or has not been divided except by abstentions — a very high degree of cohesion.

Analysis of the votes of the group by subject, as shown in Chart 14, indicates that the group has divided least on votes concerned with such issues as collective measures and regulations of armaments (3.93 per cent) and has voted identically to the greatest degree (76.5 per cent) on issues involving self-determination. The group has been divided most on issues involving the development of international law (17.3 per cent) and has voted identically least on issues concerned with international law (51.7 per cent). Considering identical votes and votes in which some of the members of the group abstain, but in which none of the group is in opposition, the group has tended to support issues involving collective measures, peaceful settlement, and human rights to a higher degree than issues involving economic, social, and humanitarian cooperation, the development of international law, and administrative, procedural, and structural matters.

Chart 15, which indicates the identical, solidarity, and divided votes of the group according to the types of recommended action, shows that the Arab caucusing group is divided least on issues recommending states to take action (6.7 per cent). The highest degree of identical voting is on votes involving recommendations that states supply funds or information.

Since there is a high degree of cohesion in the voting of the Arab group, it might be asked to what degree this cohesion places the group with the majority of the General Assembly. Chart 16 indicates, by regular sessions, the extent to which the majority of the Arab caucusing group has been in agreement with the majority of the General Assembly, the percentage of votes on which the majority of the group has abstained, with some members supporting the Assembly majority, and the extent to which the majority of the group has been in opposition to the Assembly majority. Here there is an indication that since the Xth Session the group has found itself supporting the majority of the Assembly to a slightly lesser degree than before. This trend is a bit more than is indicated by a hurried view of the chart, because the votes in the earlier sessions, especially the Third Session are peculiar to that session which was largely concerned with human rights issues, in which many of the Arab Group abstained on the crucial roll-call votes. This trend has been somewhat offset by a higher degree of abstention on issues by a majority of the group, although a few of the members supported the Assembly majority position. Evidently, when only a few of the group members support the Assembly majority, the majority of the group prefer to abstain rather than oppose other members of the group.

Considering the position of the majority of the Arab caucusing group vis-à-vis the Assembly majority according to the subject matter of votes, Chart 17 shows that the group is with the majority of the Assembly to the largest extent on matters involving such issues as collective measures and regulation of armaments (76.4 per cent). This fact may have a close relation to the fact that the group has had the least degree of divided voting in this category of votes; but there has also been a low degree of divided votes on self-determination issues, and yet the group is with the Assembly majority to a lesser degree on these issues than on most others. In any case, the group majority has supported the Assembly majority in about 60 per cent of the total votes and has been "not against" (i.e., the majority has abstained) about 75 to 80 per cent of the time.

The relation of the group majority to the Assembly majority on voting according to the type of action recommendations is shown in Chart 18. The Arab group majority has been with the Assembly majority most on issues involving recommendations that states supply funds or information. In terms of *all* action recommendations the group is with the United Nations majority about 65 to 75 per cent of the time. The significance of these percentages is more evident when Chart 18 is considered in relation to similar charts on the other groups.

To summarize, although there are inherent in its membership divisive factors which offer many parliamentary opportunities to political sophisticates, the Arab caucusing group has maintained a very high degree of cohesion in voting as compared to other caucusing groups. There has been some lessening of cohesion, especially since Iraq joined the Baghdad Pact, and it is not yet possible to say how it will be affected by the disposition of the parliamentary monarchy in Iraq; but it is clear that continued weakening of its unity would affect the whole group position. Surprisingly, group cohesion has not meant that the group has been in the United Nations majority more than 60 to 70 per cent of the time. It may be that, as in the case of the Soviet bloc, the high degree of voting cohesion — in fact, identical voting — indicates a tendency toward rigid and fixed positions which prevent any higher degree of agreement with the majority of the United Nations.

THE LATIN AMERICAN CAUCUSING GROUP

The twenty Latin American members of the United Nations have had considerable experience of joint cooperation both in the League of Nations and in the various Pan-American organizations. As a caucusing group, the Latin American states initiated their joint consultations about the United Nations in the Conference at Chapultepec early in 1945. That inter-American meeting, held before the San Francisco Conference, provided a basis of joint proposals and outlooks reflected in the Charter Conference and, ever since, behind the scenes of the United Nations.

Unlike most of the other groups in the Assembly, the Latin American caucusing group has had the same membership during the entire history of the organization. The group has consisted of:

Argentina	Dominican Republic	Nicaragua
Bolivia	Ecuador	Panama
Brazil	El Salvador	Paraguay
Chile	Guatemala	Peru
Colombia	Haiti	Uruguay
Costa Rica	Honduras	Venezuela
Cuba	Mexico	

As the United Nations membership has enlarged, the Latin American caucusing group has naturally diminished proportionally in relation to the over-all membership. Thus the group in the First Session constituted 39.3 per cent of the membership; in 1959 it constituted only 24.4 per cent.

As a result of its League experiences and the joint consulting experience at San Francisco, the group's operations have been fairly well organized ever since the first part of the First Session in 1946. Originally concerned primarily with joint consideration as to the determination of candidates for elections, the group caucus has gradually concerned itself with almost every issue before the United Nations. The Latin American delegate elected Vice-President of the General Assembly is automatically the chairman of the caucusing group. Meetings in the earlier sessions were called upon request, but since the Ninth Session the group has held regular meetings every other week. Special meetings are also held as desired. On occasion the group meetings have concerned themselves with matters of joint concern not related to the United Nations. Outsiders, such as other delegations, are often asked to appear before the group to explain their position or view on some matter before the

Assembly. The Latin American caucusing group is quite formalized in its procedure in comparison with the other groups. Decisions are taken on joint tactics and strategy on most issues before the General Assembly as well as other organs of the United Nations — although such decisions are not binding, their effectiveness depending upon the extent of support they gain within the group.

It might be argued that, apart from a fairly common historical heritage, most of the cohesive factors which unite the members of this group are their common problems. Fifteen of the twenty states are primarily dependent upon one commodity for economic stability. Most of them are dependent upon foreign trade for their economic well-being and suffer from adverse balances of payments. In turn, the dependence upon the condition of foreign markets, the one commodity economies, the low state of economic development, and the lack of extensive social development are sources of internal pressures leading in part to unstable political regimes which may shift under the influence of the changing external economic conditions.

The similarity of their problems leads to many internal competitive forces which provide fulcrums upon which outside interests can operate, and certain delegations in the Assembly exert considerable pressures on members of this group. Some Asian countries regularly have members of their delegations touring the Latin American foreign offices "lobbying" for their views. In this connection, since many of the Latin American countries are subject to fairly regular *coup d'états*, particular policy formulations are often left to individuals, and the Latin American delegates frequently have a freer set of "instructions" on issues before the United Nations than other delegations, the result is that the Latin American group, even when united in its approach, is generally flexible in its ability to work out coalitions with other groups. It can organize united support on issues which are not of vital concern to Latin America and, in return, get support for issues which are of vital joint concern to the group. Thus the group majority generally is able to adapt and adjust itself to insure that it rides with the Assembly majority on most issues, a fact that is fairly evident in viewing the voting record of the group.

As might be expected in a group as large as the Latin American group, there is a comparatively small percentage of identical voting. Chart 19, which indicates the extent of identical, solidarity, and divided voting of the group by regular sessions of the Assembly, shows that the group votes identically less than 50 per cent of the time. Over-all, the identical voting is actually 29.2 per cent. The group has divided on 35.8 per cent of the votes. There appears to have been a slight trend towards more identical and solidarity voting since the VIIIth Session, explained in part by the fact that since the IXth Session the group has been organized on a more formal basis. In part, also, it has been the result of the fact that, since the increases in the total Assembly majority have meant that the Latin American group has had a diminishing influence, the only way to increase its effectiveness has been to get a higher degree of cohesion.

Chart 20 indicates that the group has the highest degree of identical votes on matters concerned with economic, humanitarian, and social cooperation (39.1 per cent). The least degree of identical voting is in matters concerned with the development of international law (18.2 per cent). On the basis of the types of recommendations involved in votes (Chart 21) the group has the least degree of identical voting on matters recommending funds or information be supplied (25.0 per cent).

Although the voting record appears to indicate that the group has little cohesion, the fact is that the majority of the group tends to vote together most of the time. Chart 22, which shows the votes of the majority of the group in relation to the majority of the Assembly, reveals that the majority of the Latin American group have voted with the majority of the Assembly 87.6 per cent of the time; that the majority of the group abstained rather than vote against the Assembly majority in 4.4 per cent of the votes; and that the majority of the group voted against the Assembly majority only 8.0 per cent of the over-all votes. Thus the Latin American majority has a very high degree of voting with the majority of the Assembly on all issues. Considered session by session, in the IXth and Xth Sessions the group was somewhat below its previous degree of voting with the majority, but it seems by the XIth and XIIth Sessions to have resumed its position vis-à-vis the Assembly majority. In the IXth Session, the Asian-African caucusing group began to manifest itself; and in the Xth Session the increases in total Assembly membership meant that the Latin American group had to make adjustments, through coalitions with other groups, to continue its influential role in respect to the Assembly majority. The evidence is that the group has fairly successfully adjusted to these changes in the composition of the Assembly majority.

The record of voting interpreted by subject (Chart 23) indicates that in matters concerned with self-determination the group votes with the Assembly majority only 75.0 per cent of the time, while on all other types of subjects the group votes better than 90 per cent of the time with the Assembly majority. This fact explains the voting of the group in the IXth Session, when there were more votes in the self-determination category than in any other.

Chart 24 indicates that the group has voted with the Assembly majority to a slightly higher degree on issues recommending that states act or that states supply funds or information than in recommendations for other types of action.

The correlation of the majority of the Latin American group to the Assembly majority suggests several significant facts. First, the group is large enough so that most other groups in the Assembly have to negotiate with it; and since the twenty-vote bargaining power of the group is sufficient to work compromises involving the group's attitudes negotiation usually results in some sort of agreement which gets the support of the majority of the group. Secondly, since the group is not hard and fast, it can constantly adapt itself to changing conditions — in contrast to the Soviet bloc and the Arab caucusing group, with their rigidity of position. This latter point is particularly true because of the fact that it appears to most observers that Latin American delegates have a much "freer" hand in contrast to the majority of the other delegates who operate under "closer" control of their foreign offices. One might argue further that the Latin American group has been extremely capable in its ability to maintain itself with the Assembly majority in spite of the fact that the Assembly has increased and the bloc and group picture has undergone significant changes since the first sessions, in which the Latin American group was the dominant element in any decision.

Lastly, some question might be raised as to which members of the Latin American group tend to deviate most from the group majority. It would be quite misleading to give exact percentages on the deviations because they are explained by several varying and sometimes inconsistent elements. In those Latin American states where constant fluctuations in internal political forces leave a great deal of foreign policy formulation in the hands of the delegates to the Assembly, a change in the delegates may present shifts in policy that mean a higher degree of deviation from the group. In other cases, the deviations may be on the basis of peculiar circumstances which would not warrant generalization. On an over-all basis, however, it appears that Mexico, Guatemala, Argentina, Bolivia, and Costa Rica — in that order — are more likely to deviate from the group majority, particularly if the group majority is supporting the general position of the United States and the western powers. The extent of deviation in the group is not great, and there appears to be little pattern to it.

THE COMMONWEALTH CAUCUSING GROUP

The Commonwealth has had a wealth of consultative experience which has been carried over into the United Nations. Prior to the San Francisco Conference, the Commonwealth Prime Ministers met in May 1944 to discuss the future world organization, and representatives of the Commonwealth countries held consultations in London in April 1945, just before the Charter Conference, and during the San Francisco Conference. Such Commonwealth group meetings have continued behind the scenes of the General Assembly ever since.

Since the Commonwealth caucusing group membership has included only those members of the Commonwealth, also members of the United Nations, the number of independent members of the Commonwealth has increased and the group has grown from six to ten. It will be noted from the following outline of its evolution that not only the number but also the complexion of the group has changed.

General Assembly Sessions I (1) through S-I —
1946 to 29 September 1947

| (6) | Australia | India | South Africa |
| | Canada | New Zealand | United Kingdom |

General Assembly Sessions II through X —
September 1947 to 14 December 1955

(7)	Australia	New Zealand	South Africa
	Canada	Pakistan	United Kingdom
	India		

General Assembly Sessions X through First Part of XI —
14 December 1955 to 8 March 1957

(8)	Australia	India	South Africa
	Canada	New Zealand	United Kingdom
	Ceylon	Pakistan	

General Assembly Sessions XI (Second Part) —
8 March 1957 to 17 September 1957

(9)	Australia	Ghana	Pakistan
	Canada	India	South Africa
	Ceylon	New Zealand	United Kingdom

General Assembly Session XII to present — 17 Sept. 1957 to present

(10)	Australia	India	Pakistan
	Canada	Malaya	South Africa
	Ceylon	New Zealand	United Kingdom
	Ghana		

The Commonwealth caucusing group is essentially a consultation group. It meets generally once a week while the Assembly is in session, the meetings being quite informal and providing usually

only a basis for an exchange of views. Issues which reflect a fundamental cleavage in the group are rarely considered. The group may
also meet at the request of any of its members for a special meeting.
Some efforts are made to reach a consensus on the issues before the
group, and efforts are often made to get members to abstain on an
issue if they feel that they cannot support the group consensus; but
it remains a diverse group, interested in a common strategy where
it is possible to agree, but in no sense a hard-and-fast organization.

The Commonwealth itself provides the ties between the group —
not simply loose political ties but also economic ties of integrated
trade and the sterling area. Historically, the common background
of political experience has laid the basis for many common features
of law and political organization, but these are offset by the individual natures of the various members such as a Hindu India, Moslem Pakistan, apartheid South Africa, and socialist New Zealand.
Generally, Ceylon, India, and Ghana appear to be at "odds," with
the group; South Africa is seldom in harmony with any faction
within the group. Far from cohesive in its voting, the group presents
a picture of fairly individualist action on any issues on which particular members may have strong convictions.

The voting record of the Commonwealth group provides considerable evidence as to the looseness of its organization.

With the exception of the First Part of the First Session (concerned primarily with organizational matters), the group has had
a very low degree of either identical or solidarity votes until the
Xth Session, when the degree of identical and solidarity voting increased markedly (Chart 25). This appears to be the result of the
fact that the number of votes essentially concerned with self-determination matters dropped from a norm of about 25 per cent over-all
votes up to the Xth Session to about 10 per cent of the votes in the
later sessions. On an over-all basis for the first thirteen years, the
Commonwealth group has voted identically 13.1 per cent of the
time and has been divided 58.4 per cent of the time.

Considered by subject (Chart 26), voting by the Commonwealth
group surprisingly has been identical most often on matters in-

volving economic, social, and humanitarian cooperation (41.4 per cent). The group has had the lowest degree of identical voting on issues involving human rights issues (3.4 per cent), which fact further substantiates the over-all voting trend since the Xth Session. Considering the character of the membership of the group, it is apparent that, although there is disagreement on self-determination matters, the common benefits of economic and similar cooperation constitute an area of mutual interest. On recommendations other than for action by states the group has a much higher degree of identical votes (19.7 per cent) than on issues recommending that states appropriate funds or supply information (7.16 per cent) as Chart 27 shows.

Viewing the voting of the majority of the Commonwealth group with the majority of the General Assembly in regular sessions (Chart 28), we see that the group has been in the majority of the United Nations between 65 and 70 per cent of the time on all issues. Up to the VIth Session there was a fairly steady decrease in the voting with the Assembly majority. The VIth Session registered the lowest agreement of the group majority with the Assembly majority, perhaps because in that session there were many votes involving human rights and self-determination. Some explanation of this session is provided by the fact that on these issues Australia, Canada, New Zealand, and the United Kingdom, and in many instances South Africa, constituted a majority of the group against India and Pakistan, and this majority within the group was in opposition to the Assembly majority.

The record of voting by subject (Chart 29) shows that the Commonwealth group voted with Assembly majority to the greatest degree in issues involving administrative, procedural, and structural matters, and matters concerned with economic, social, and cultural cooperation. The group majority supported the Assembly majority least on issues involving human rights. Chart 30 shows that the group majority supported the Assembly majority about equally on recommendations that states should take certain actions and that actions be taken by other organs. The group supported the Assembly majority least on recommendations that states appropriate funds or supply information.

The voting record viewed as a whole confirms the impression that the Commonwealth caucusing group is not a hard and fast group but a very loose one. It seems to comprise several factions none of which in itself is closely unified. On many issues India, Pakistan, Ceylon, Ghana, and Malaya seem opposed to the other members. Of these five, Pakistan and Malaya are more likely to support the positions of the United Kingdom, Australia, Canada, and New Zealand than are Ceylon, Ghana, and India. On many issues South Africa finds itself alone and in opposition to the group. It is too soon after the admission of Ghana and Malaya to be certain just what their role in the group will be. A detailed analysis of the voting of this group in the XIIIth Session would illustrate the fact that the fairly even division of this group means that with abstentions either one of the factions or the other which takes a position puts the group minority in the majority of the Assembly. Thus far, the greatest unanimity in the group has been demonstrated in the procedural role of selecting its candidates for elective posts in the United Nations.

THE SCANDINAVIAN CAUCUSING GROUP

A unified approach to international organization by the Scandinavian states was first concertedly developed in the League of Nations. In 1945 there was close cooperation between Norway and Denmark at the San Francisco United Nations Conference, and with the admission of Sweden and Iceland to the United Nations in the Second Part of the First Session in November 1946 the present caucusing group of four members came into regular operation. Although Finland was admitted to the United Nations in 1955, it does not appear that Finland is actually a member of what might be called the Scandinavian caucusing group. Finland, under considerable pressure by its neighbor the Soviet Union, has consultations with the other Scandinavian states but did not join the Nordic Council until October 1956 and appeared to be "allied" for "geographical distribution" reasons with the East European countries. Until Finland has been a member of the United Nations for several more sessions it will not be possible accurately to evaluate its voting.

Prior to each session of the General Assembly, deliberations are held by the Scandinavian governments on the items on the provisional agenda. Problems that arise in these consultations are considered in the regular meetings of the foreign ministers. Both tactics and strategy on procedural and substantive issues are discussed, and efforts are made to reach a common position. During the Assembly sessions regular joint meetings are held by the delegations of the group on most of the important issues; these meetings are directed toward reaching a common ground but are not formalized in procedure.

The four Scandinavian states in the group have a broad basis for common action and outlook in their geographical proximity, strong cultural ties, a similarity of languages, the existence of similar democratic political systems, and the experience of long-term consultations and cooperation on many social and economic matters. Despite their failure to reach an agreement on some form of a common defensive pact in 1950, cooperation in other fields resulted in the establishment of the Nordic Council in 1952–1953; and only in the field of defense consultation have external influences outweighed the desires for mutual cooperation. Norway, Denmark, and Iceland have joined the North Atlantic Treaty Organization. Sweden, which has pushed for a regional arrangement without external associations, has continued to maintain its policy of armed neutrality.

As a general practice the members of the Scandinavian group do not vote against each other. If they do not vote identically, they tend to abstain rather than express opposition to each other. Chart 31 indicates that, while the over-all identical votes are 68.4 per cent, the members of the group have so consistently abstained rather than vote against each other that they are "not opposed" to each other 92.7 per cent of the time. The chart also indicates that since the beginning of the IXth Session the group has been divided about 15 per cent of the time while prior to the IXth Session it was divided on only about 6 per cent of the votes. This sudden increase in the number of divided votes is explained by the increasing number of votes on Chinese representation in the General Assembly since the beginning of the IXth Session. On this issue Iceland has voted with the United States; and Denmark, Norway, and Sweden have voted with those members who favor unseating the representatives of Nationalist China and replacing them with representatives from Communist China.

Analyzing the vote according to the types of subjects involved in the votes (Chart 32) indicates that the group has divided the most on procedural issues (13.2 per cent), development of international law (12.1 per cent), and human rights (7.1 per cent). The comparatively "high" division on procedural issues is attributable to the divided attitudes of the Scandinavian group on the question of Chinese representation (a procedural matter). The group is not divided at all on collective measures issues, and it is divided less than 4 per cent of the time on peaceful settlement, self-determination, and economic, social, and humanitarian cooperation issues. Looking at the types of recommendations involved in the votes, (Chart 33) we see that the group is divided least on recommendations that states take certain actions (4.7 per cent) — although this is not very different from the voting of the group on other types of recommendations.

On an over-all basis, the Scandinavian group majority votes with the Assembly majority 68.7 per cent of the time, and against the majority of the General Assembly 20.8 per cent of the time (Chart 34). The group majority abstains rather than opposes the majority of the General Assembly only 11.5 per cent of the time, an indication that, although the members of the group will abstain rather than oppose each other, the group does not often abstain rather than oppose the majority of the Assembly. This fact reflects the rather independent attitude of the Scandinavian group, which tends to support its position regardless of pressures from the Assembly majority. Looking at the votes in the regular session, there seems to be little pattern to the fluctuations in the percentages of votes of the group in agreement with the Assembly majority. For example, the large percentage of votes against the Assembly majority in the IVth Session is explained by the opposition of the group majority to a series of votes on the question of Jerusalem and to votes on aspects of a convention on the suppression of traffic in women and children.

On the basis of the subject of the votes, Chart 35 shows that the Scandinavian group majority votes with the majority of the General Assembly most on issues involving collective measures (80.0 per cent) and against the Assembly majority most on issues involving the development of international law (33.3 per cent). The group indicates little difference in its voting on issues according to the types of recommendations involved in the votes (Chart 36).

THE BENELUX CAUCUSING GROUP

The three Benelux countries, Belgium, Netherlands, and Luxembourg, seem to have worked as a group throughout the history of the General Assembly. On many occasions the group view is presented before the Assembly by a spokesman for the group. The consultations of the group appear to be rather informal and to have their base in the extensive cooperation between these three states which has steadily gained impetus since the middle of the Second World War. In September 1943 the representatives of the three exiled governments signed a preliminary monetary agreement which envisioned further plans of peacetime cooperation between their countries. Initially this cooperation was confined to matters of economics and finance; as time went on, it encompassed most areas of activity.

Many difficulties were encountered in developing the economic union which had its formal beginnings in 1951, a large share of them being due to different economic approaches by Belgium and the Netherlands, which in turn responded differently to outside pressures; and there have been other "disputes" among the countries, such as those on problems related to the waterways and the continual competition between Antwerp and Rotterdam as ports. Nevertheless, the economic integration of the three countries has gradually advanced, and in turn the three countries have felt that it must be sustained by cooperation on all issues. That cooperation has extended into the United Nations, and the frequent consultations between the three countries justify its existence as a caucusing group. Since 1956 this group has operated as a unit within the slightly larger Western European caucusing group. As a whole, it has displayed a high degree of cohesion in the General Assembly.

The Benelux Group has voted identically on 77.7 per cent of the votes over all the sessions and has been divided only 5.4 per cent of the time (Chart 37). Members of the group as a rule abstain rather than oppose each other. Issues involving procedure or the development of international law appear to be those on which the group is most likely to be divided (Chart 38), but such divisions are less than 10 per cent. Likewise, there appears to be little significant difference in the divisions of the group on votes according to the types of recommended actions at votes (Chart 39), where the degree of division is very small.

On the over-all basis, the Benelux group has been in the Assembly majority 69.9 per cent of the time (Chart 40) and has opposed the majority of the General Assembly 22.3 per cent of the time. It will be noted that the group allied itself less and less frequently with those forming the majority until after the VIIth Session, and that since that time it has been increasingly in coalition with the majority. The apparent reversal of the group voting trend is explained in part by the fact that, as the Asian-African group has developed since the Vth and VIth Sessions, those opposed to it, especially on matters concerned with human rights and self-determination, have begun to form coalitions against the Asian-African group in order to "control" the Assembly majority. The Benelux group has in the over-all disagreed with the Assembly majority most on issues involving self-determination and human rights (Chart 41) and on recommendations concerned with appropriating funds or supplying information (Chart 42).

As a very small consulting group, the Benelux group has been fairly effective in the General Assembly, not only in playing a fairly united role but also in the contribution of its representatives, several of whom have served as Presidents of the General Assembly. In addition, most of the representatives of this group play a very active role behind the scenes in the Assembly in the negotiations between groups and in facilitating agreements between the caucusing groups.

THE ASIAN-AFRICAN CAUCUSING GROUP

Since 1946 the percentage of Asian and African members of the United Nations has increased from 23.5 per cent to 36.6 per cent of the total membership. Prior to 1950 most of the Asian-African members were Arab states forming their own caucusing group. Since that time there has been a steady increase in non-Arab Asian-African members representing a much broader base of shared interests, a development which is the simplest explanation for the formation of the very large present Asian-African caucusing group. In addition to internal factors naturally encouraging a large Asian-African grouping in the United Nations, the early domination of the Assembly by Western Europe and Latin America made it increasingly necessary for the Asian and African states to organize if they were to have any chance of being effective, especially as the Assembly began to concern itself more and more with issues such as self-determination which are of vital concern to the Asian and African members. Thus, beginning in 1949 and 1950, some of the Asian-African members not in the Arab caucusing group organized on an *ad hoc* basis; and, after the Bandung Conference in 1955, the more formal Asian-African caucusing group was organized starting with the Xth Session.

The history of the present Asian-African caucusing group begins, then, with the nucleus which met formally, on an *ad hoc* basis, during the Vth Session as a group of twelve, consisting of Afghanistan, Burma, Egypt, India, Indonesia, Iran, Iraq, Lebanon, Pakistan,

Saudi Arabia, Syria, and Yemen. Following the failure of the Assembly to agree upon the disposition of the former Italian colonies during the Third Session, Sir Benegal Rau of India called the first meeting of this group in the fall of 1949 to see if they could work out a basis of compromise on this issue. The group was successful in finding the basis for settlement on this issue which was one of the only issues ever referred to the Assembly in such a manner that the Assembly could make a final decision instead of simply recommending a settlement. This initial success laid the beginnings for the group, at least on an *ad hoc* basis. In the Vth Session this initial group, generally called the "Arab-Asian Group," concerned itself primarily with efforts to mediate the Korean dispute under the leadership of the Indian delegate, Sir Benegal Rau, who acted as their agent in behind-the-scenes negotiations. China with its Nationalist representatives, Ethiopia, Liberia, the Philippines, Thailand, and Turkey, the other Asian and African countries, were not included in this initial group.

The group came into being again in the VIth Session, initially with respect to the French-Tunisian question, but rapidly expanded its area of concern to other "mutual problems" and exercised its joint concern not only in activities of the General Assembly but also in meetings of the Disarmament Commission and the Human Rights Commission of the Economic and Social Council. The "psychological and moral" success of this *ad hoc* group was such that Liberia and Ethiopia, although not formally drawn into the group, cooperated with it on several occasions. The Philippines was formally brought into this group at this time as a participating member. Because of an internal split within the group over tactics on the French-Tunisian issue, Syria and Lebanon withdrew from the group during this session. Nationalist China, which at no time has been a formal member, approached the group during the VIth Session, indicated a desire to support their caucus "decisions," and was "informally" made aware of the group inclinations. At no time since has Nationalist China been in any formal or informal contact with the group actions, though obviously the Chinese delegates can gather by "observation" the position and concerns of the group.

During the VIIth and VIIIth Sessions the group was again constituted on an *ad hoc* basis and continued to concern itself only with those issues of common concern that were before the General Assembly. During both of these sessions, Syria and Lebanon rejoined the group meetings. In the IXth Session Thailand joined the group when it was once again brought into being on an *ad hoc* consultative basis, and Ethiopia and Liberia were brought into a more "direct relationship" with the group.

Considerable common interest as the result of the fact that most of them had won their independence around the time of the beginning of the United Nations served as an important factor in bringing the Asian-African countries into consultation. The formation of the Arab League in 1945 brought the Arab members of the group together. An unofficial Asian Relations Conference in New Delhi in March 1947 brought many of the national leaders of these countries together. The Dutch action against the newly created Republic of Indonesia led to the Delhi Conference (of 15 Asian states) on Indonesia in January 1949, which agreed on joint representations to the United Nations. This Delhi Conference appears to have laid the basis for consultation which was subsequently begun in 1949 and 1950 under the impetus of Sir Benegal Rau behind the scenes at the United Nations. A conference called in Baguio in the Philippines (May 1950) brought six Asian members together where they agreed to "act in consultation with each other through normal diplomatic channels to further the interest of the peoples of this region . . . [and to] seek joint action so as to exercise due influence in the United Nations, its specialized agencies and other international organizational organizations. . . ." The Baguio Conference included representatives from Australia, Ceylon, India, Pakistan, the Philippines, Thailand, and Indonesia.

At the invitation of the Prime Minister of Ceylon, the Prime Ministers of India, Pakistan, Ceylon, Burma, and Indonesia met in Colombo in April 1954. This Conference concentrated upon issues of wide international concern, such as the situation in Indo-China, the hydrogen bomb, the problem of the representation of Communist China in the United Nations, colonialism in general, the issues of Tunisia and Morocco before the United Nations, the problems of Arab refugees, and economic cooperation. This conference also considered a suggestion from the Indonesian Premier that a conference of Asian and African states be held. Subsequent negotiations by the Indonesian Premier led to a further meeting of these "Colombo Powers" in Bogor in December 1954, where the five states considered the composition and agenda for the proposed conference. It was agreed that its purpose would be to consider problems of special interest to Asian and African peoples and to view the position of their countries in the world and the contribution they could make to the promotion of peace and international cooperation. On this basis, invitations were extended to all the independent states of Asia and Africa except South Africa, North Korea, South Korea, Israel, and Nationalist China.

As a consequence of the Bogor Conference invitation the Bandung Conference met in April 1955. It was attended by representatives from Afghanistan, Cambodia, Chinese People's Republic, Egypt, Ethiopia, Gold Coast (Ghana), Iran, Iraq, Japan, Jordan, Laos, Lebanon, Liberia, Libya, Nepal, Philippines, Saudi Arabia, Sudan, Syria, Thailand, Turkey, North Viet Nam, South Viet Nam, and Yemen in addition to the five sponsoring countries, Burma, Ceylon, India, Indonesia, and Pakistan. Of the twenty-nine countries, seventeen were at that time members of the United Nations. The Conference considered a broad agenda covering economic cooperation, cultural cooperation, human rights and self-determination, problems of dependent peoples, and promotion of world peace and cooperation.

Without going into details of the conference and its discussions, all of which are pertinent to a complete understanding of the Asian-African attitudes in the United Nations, several significant points should be noted here. The conference was conducted in such a way as to stress the issues of common concern and to minimize any inherent conflicts. In a general sense the major theme advanced was that under present world tensions much could be gained by viewing Asia and Africa as a unity, and that mutual consultation and cooperation between the Asian and African countries should rest on this theme as a base. Moreover, in the words of the Conference, "The problem of peace is correlative with the problems of international security. In this connection, *all* States should cooperate, especially *through the United Nations. . . .*" (Italics added). A reading of the records of the Conference proceedings also suggests that inherent in the desire for common consultation was the implication that such consultation should extend to the members of the Bandung Conference regardless of whether they were members of the United Nations.

As a result of the Bandung Conference, the Asian-African group was formally organized as a caucusing group in the General Assembly in the Xth Session, and included all seventeen Asian and African states then members of the United Nations. The group was enlarged in the XIth Session with the admission of Cambodia, Ceylon, Japan, Jordan, Laos, Libya, Morocco, Tunisia, Nepal, and Sudan. The subsequent admissions of Ghana and Malaya gave the Asian-African caucusing group a membership total of 29 in the XIIth Session which was reduced to 28 with the unification of Egypt and Syria into the United Arab Republic in 1958. With the admission of Guinea late in the XIIIth session the total was again raised to 29.

Viewed session by session, then, the membership of the Asian-African caucusing group has been as follows:

General Assembly Session V — 1950 (ad hoc basis):

(12)	Afghanistan	Indonesia	Pakistan
	Burma	Iran	Saudi Arabia
	Egypt	Iraq	Syria
	India	Lebanon	Yemen

General Assembly Session VI — 1951 (ad hoc basis):

(11)	Afghanistan	Indonesia	Philippines
	Burma	Iran	Saudi Arabia
	Egypt	Iraq	Yemen
	India	Pakistan	

General Assembly Sessions VII and VIII — 1952 and 1953 (ad hoc basis):

(13)
Afghanistan	Iran	Saudi Arabia
Burma	Iraq	Syria
Egypt	Lebanon	Yemen
India	Pakistan	
Indonesia	Philippines	

General Assembly Session IX — 1954 (ad hoc basis):

(14)
Afghanistan	Iran	Saudi Arabia
Burma	Iraq	Syria
Egypt	Lebanon	Thailand
India	Pakistan	Yemen
Indonesia	Philippines	

General Assembly Session X — 1955 (regular basis):

(17)
Afghanistan	Iran	Saudi Arabia
Burma	Iraq	Syria
Egypt	Lebanon	Thailand
Ethiopia	Liberia	Turkey
India	Pakistan	Yemen
Indonesia	Philippines	

General Assembly Session XI — 1956 (regular basis):

(27)
Afghanistan	Iraq	Pakistan
Burma	Japan	Philippines
Cambodia	Jordan	Saudi Arabia
Ceylon	Laos	Sudan
Egypt	Lebanon	Syria
Ethiopia	Liberia	Thailand
India	Libya	Tunisa
Indonesia	Morocco	Turkey
Iran	Nepal	Yemen

General Assembly Session XII — 1957 (regular basis):

(29)
Afghanistan	India	Lebanon
Burma	Indonesia	Liberia
Cambodia	Iran	Libya
Ceylon	Iraq	Malaya
Egypt	Japan	Morocco
Ethiopia	Jordan	Nepal
Ghana	Laos	Pakistan

Philippines	Syria	Turkey
Saudi Arabia	Thailand	Yemen
Sudan	Tunisia	

General Assembly 3rd Special Session until later part of the XIIIth
Session — 8 August 1958 to 12 December 1958 (Regular Basis)

(28)

Afghanistan	Japan	Philippines
Burma	Jordan	Saudi Arabia
Cambodia	Laos	Sudan
Ceylon	Lebanon	Thailand
Ethiopia	Liberia	Tunisia
Ghana	Libya	Turkey
India	Malaya	United Arab Republic
Indonesia	Morocco	Yemen
Iran	Nepal	
Iraq	Pakistan	

General Assembly Session XIII (later part) to present —
12 December 1958-1959 (regular basis)

(29)

Afghanistan	Iraq	Pakistan
Burma	Japan	Philippines
Cambodia	Jordan	Saudi Arabia
Ceylon	Laos	Sudan
Ethiopia	Lebanon	Thailand
Ghana	Liberia	Tunisia
Guinea	Libya	Turkey
India	Malaya	United Arab Republic
Indonesia	Morocco	Yemen
Iran	Nepal	

The Asian-African group meets regularly, not only when the
General Assembly is in session but also during the rest of the year
as the need arises, and meetings may be called at the request of
any member who desires to consult with the group. Since generally
the meetings are confined to those issues on which the majority
of the group has a common view, the group does not consult on
all issues before the General Assembly. It has been a practice of
the group not to hold meetings on any issues which involve a conflict between members of the group. For example the group has
never considered the Kashmir dispute between India and Pakistan.

The only exception to this "harmonizing" rule was in 1958 when the group did hold meetings to consider the situation in Lebanon. The group has a system of rotating chairmen and is quite informal in its procedures. Although votes (which are not binding) may be taken at the meetings, efforts are directed usually at reaching an informal consensus. It follows that for the most part the meetings serve as "sounding boards." They tend to be brief; delegates may explain their views on an issue without further discussion, or ideas may be tossed out for the purpose of seeing whether it is possible to reach agreement on common attitudes, tactics, or strategy within the limitations imposed by instructions from their foreign offices. Meetings are not restricted to the heads of delegations but are often attended by other members of the delegations and in many respects are quite open. On occasion the meetings are attended by other parties. For example representatives of the Algerian National Liberation Front have participated with the group in discussions on the Algerian question. The group does not appoint Assembly spokesmen for their views as does the Latin American caucusing group.

In a real sense, the important function of the Asian-African group is to bring its members together formally so that those having special interests in common can consult conveniently. In this sense the group might be considered to have certain factions which operate within it, factions which are not hard and fast but represent poles within the group. If the experiences of the enlarged group operating in the XIth, XIIth, and XIIIth Sessions prove to be typical, two members, India and Japan, operate as polar states within the group. India is rather close to Ceylon, Indonesia, Burma, and Ghana. Japan appears to be close to Thailand, the Philippines, and some of the Middle Eastern states. At the same time, there are other poles of separation; the Arab states have their own caucusing group, and the African states organized their own caucusing group in the XIIIth Session.

The Asian-African group, including as it does most of the poorer and less developed countries of the world, consists of countries containing virtually half of the world's population, countries which are nonwhite and many of which share bitter recollections of colonialism. "It is probably correct to say that, in general, they shared a common abhorrence of imperialism, whether Western or Communist. Also, it may be safe to say that they shared a common hope and desire for economic development and social progress. These aspirations stem from a common historical experience." [13] The fact that the group has for most of its experience in the United Nations been frustrated in its efforts by the combination of the other caucusing groups, excepting the Soviet bloc, has also given the Asian-African states a sense of unity.

Aside from these general bases for unity, it is apparent that there are many divisive factors working to prevent a really effective unity within it. The group includes countries like India, Indonesia, and Burma, which pursue "neutralist" foreign policies, and countries which belong to collective security arrangements. Turkey belongs to the North Atlantic Treaty Organization. Turkey, Iran, and Pakistan belong to the Baghdad Pact. Pakistan, Thailand, and the Philippines belong to the Southeast Asian Treaty Organization, and Japan and the Philippines have common defense arrangements with the United States. Nine of the eleven Arab states belong to the Arab League. Five members of the group are also members of the Commonwealth. In addition, there are many conflicts between members of the group. India and Pakistan are split over the issue of Kashmir. Some of the members recognize Communist China, others continue their relationship with Nationalist China. Pakistan and Afghanistan are at odds over the Pushtun problem. The United Arab Republic is at odds with Jordan and Lebanon. Thailand has boundary problems with Cambodia. Burma and Ghana have economic ties with Israel, while the Arab League states are opposed to the very existence of Israel. Many other "conflicts" could be mentioned, all of which appear to give the Asian-African group the appearance of an "unholy alliance."

[13] Carlos P. Romulo, *The Meaning of Bandung* (Chapel Hill: University of North Carolina Press, 1956), p. 3.

Nevertheless, when one examines the voting record of the Asian-African caucusing group, it becomes apparent that, although it presents a far from united voting record, considering the size of the group and its opposition to most of the other groups, it has been fairly effective in "going with the Assembly majority." This is in large part due to the fact that the group makes a very conscious effort to stress harmony by not holding meetings on issues involving disputes between group members thus preventing animosities from spreading to the other issues upon which the group might find common ground. Chart 43 indicates that since the beginnings of the group on an *ad hoc* basis in the Vth Session the group has been divided to a lesser degree than it was before the Vth Session. The identical votes have increased only slightly, but the group has increased its solidarity voting considerably, which is particularly significant considering the large size of the group. The high degree of cohesion in the VIIIth Session reflects the fact that the majority of roll-call votes at this session were on issues essentially involving questions of self-determination and human rights upon which the group is generally in agreement.

Examining the over-all votes of these Asian and African countries before and after the group began operating clearly shows the advantage these countries have gained by forming a caucusing group.[14] Prior to its formation members voted against each other 53.9 per cent; since the group has been organized they have divided on 23.6 per cent of the votes. Prior to organization they voted identically only 11.4 per cent of the time; since the group has been in operation they have voted identically 33.4 per cent. With the large increase in membership, identical voting has declined, but the impact of the group caucus is reflected in the fact that the consultations

[14] In compiling the voting of the group after it was formed, only those Asian and African countries which belong to the group in each session are included in the tabulations. In the votes prior to the formation of the group, all the Asian and African states that were members of the United Nations except Nationalist China and Israel were included in the tabulations. By the Xth Session, of course, the group included all the Asian and African countries except Nationalist China and Israel.

have encouraged abstentions rather than oppositions and the level of solidarity voting which rose from 34.6 per cent to 43.0 per cent, has been maintained.

The advantages derived from formation of the caucusing group become even more clear when the before-and-after voting is analyzed according to subject (Charts 44 and 45). On collective measures identical voting increased from 18.2 per cent to 35.8 per cent. It increased from 2.9 per cent to 34.2 per cent on peaceful settlement issues, from 14.0 per cent to 39.5 per cent on self-determination matters, 11.8 per cent to 28.6 per cent on economic, social, and humanitarian cooperation issues, 0.0 per cent to 40.0 per cent on human rights matters, 9.1 per cent to 13.7 per cent on issues relating to the development of international law, and 18.2 per cent to 25.7 per cent on issues concerned with administrative, procedural, or structural issues. With the exception of the votes relating to the development of international law, there has been a corresponding decrease in divided votes. Divided votes decreased from 27.6 per cent to 5.1 per cent in collective measures issues, from 54.2 per cent to 34.4 per cent in peaceful settlement matters, 59.4 per cent to 24.4 per cent in self-determination issues, 37.5 per cent to 12.5 per cent in human rights matters, 53.0 per cent to 50.0 per cent in economic, social and humanitarian issues, and 70.5 per cent to 38.9 per cent in matters concerned with administration, procedure, or structure.

The slight change in divided votes on economic, social, and humanitarian matters is related to the fact that there were many more roll-call votes on these matters percentage-wise in the early sessions than in the latter sessions, where the general consensus on these issues forced votes primarily on issues where there were strongly divided opinions. The increased division on issues related to the development of international law, may well be due to the fact that such votes often involve technical matters of little political importance on which there is no strong group incentive to unite. The main concerns of the group are on matters relating to self-determination, human rights, and collective measures, and the caucus meetings exert a greater degree of influence in these areas than in any other with the exception of procedural matters related to matters of primary concern. Chart 45 indicates that the group has demonstrated its greatest degree of cohesiveness on these two subjects and on votes related to human rights and peaceful settlement.

Analyzed according to the types of recommendations, the before-and-after voting record again shows increases in identical voting and decreases in divided voting (Charts 46 and 47). The biggest changes occurred with respect to votes recommending that states take action and recommendations that other action be taken, the least noticeable in votes recommending that states appropriate funds or supply information. In the latter category divided votes decreased only slightly, and there was a decrease in identical voting after the formation of the group.

Chart 48, showing the relationship of the majority of the Asian-African group with the majority of the Assembly, and including the voting of the Asian and African countries in the sessions before the caucusing group was organized, indicates that there has been only a slight change in that relationship since the organization of the caucusing group in the Vth Session. Before the Vth Session members of the group opposed the Assembly majority on 22.9 per cent of the votes; since the formation of the group its majority has opposed the Assembly majority 15.2 per cent. (This figure, based not only on the votes in the regular sessions but also on those in the special sessions, is not completely evident from Chart 48.) There is a contrast here with the other large caucusing group, the Latin American group, which has been in the majority of the Assembly generally more than 90 per cent of the time — interesting evidence of the fact that there is a tendency of the Asian-African states to find themselves opposed by the Assembly majority which is a cohesive factor uniting the Asian-African group.

The opposition of the majority of the Asian-African caucusing group to the Assembly majority is delineated more precisely in Charts 49 and 50. Prior to the organization of the caucus the majority of the Asian and African countries voted identically most often on issues involving peaceful settlement and international law, and least on issues involving human rights and collective measures. In both categories the majority of the group abstained to a high degree rather than vote against the Assembly majority. Since the formation of the caucusing group, however, the group majority has been with the Assembly majority most often on issues involving collective measures, issues related to procedure, and matters related to the development of international law. The group majority has been most often in disagreement with the Assembly majority on matters involving economic, social, and humanitarian cooperation, self-determination, and human rights — all subjects which are of considerable mutual interest to the group.

An analysis of the votes according to types of recommendations both before and after the formation of the group indicates an interesting shift (Charts 51 and 52). Prior to the formation of the caucus the majority of the members opposed the Assembly majority most frequently on votes involving recommendations that states appropriate funds or supply information. Since the formation of the Asian-African group it is this category in which the group majority opposes the Assembly majority least.

From the foregoing outline of its voting history it seems fairly apparent that the organization of the Asian-African caucusing group has made significant changes in the relations of its members with the Assembly. On subjects in which they have common interests they have increased both their identical and solidarity voting; and it is precisely on these subjects that the group finds itself most in opposition to the Assembly majority. Considering the multitude of divisive forces in the group, the extent of identical votes is significant; and it would be misleading to assume that the large size and varied membership of the group render it ineffective.

These facts raise significant questions as to the future character of bloc politics in the General Assembly. If the Asian-African group continues its consultations over a period of time and at the same time continues to find itself in opposition to the Assembly majority on certain subjects, will this mean that the group will gain further unity and its identical voting increase? Will it achieve sufficient unity to be able to press for divisions in other groups which could transform the nature of the Assembly majority and place the Asian-African group with the majority instead of the opposition? On the other hand, if those now in the Assembly majority foster the inherent divisive elements in this group, can the present factions within it be tempted to split from the group?

It needs to be remembered that successful votes in the General Assembly require not a simple majority or two-thirds majority, but the largest possible majority, if they are to be effective. The Asian-African group as now constituted, when it is united and identical, or nearly identical, in voting, can prevent the Assembly from passing issues with an overwhelming majority, if not actually defeat the majority. It is therefore already in a strong position to urge other groups to consider the desirability of making concessions and any concessions made for the sake of achieving overwhelming majorities may well serve to strengthen the cohesion and effectiveness of those receiving them. Leaders of the Asian-African caucusing group cannot be unaware of these facts.

THE WESTERN EUROPEAN CAUCUSING GROUP

Common cooperative efforts reflected in the growing experiences of the European Coal and Steel Community, the European Atomic Energy Community, and the newly formed European Common Market, as well as the larger Western European Union, have brought about a close relationship among five members of the United Nations: Belgium, France, Italy, Luxembourg, and The Netherlands; and after the admission of Italy, in 1955, these states formed a Western European caucusing group which has been operative since the XIth Session in 1956. In its operation this group is very similar to the Benelux and Scandinavian groups. Consultations are held both before the Assembly meets and fairly regularly during the sessions, and the delegates in this group, quite perceptive to the uses of political-interest groups, appear to have been fairly effective in using their joint efforts to ensure that the group coalitions which have dominated the Assembly majority continue to play such a role.

It is too soon to judge the long-term strength of this group. Its members share elements of common historical development, similar political organization, and regional organizational ties; but the group is characterized by a strong flavor of nationalistic feeling. In France and Italy particularly the fractionization of political parties enhances the possibility that alterations in the governing coalitions may place obstacles in the way of developing cohesive political ties, as has happened on several occasions since the Second World War.

An examination of the voting record indicates that thus far the organization of the group has increased the unity of its members in the General Assembly. They have been divided less than previously, and they have voted identically to a higher degree (Chart 53). On the basis of the over-all total votes, these states voted identically 65.0 per cent of the time before the formation of the group whereas since the operation of the group they have voted identically on 79.0 per cent of the votes, a significant increase. Prior to the organization of the group they divided on 11.2 per cent of the votes; since the group came into being they have divided on only 7.2 per cent of the votes.

Prior to formation of the group they voted identically most on economic, social, and humanitarian issues (80 per cent) and least on collective measures (51.1 per cent); on all other issues they voted identically 66 per cent to 75 per cent of the time. Since the formation of the group they have voted identically most on issues relating to the development of international law (100 per cent), self-determination (90 per cent), and collective measures (83.0 per cent). Since the group was formed they have voted identically least on peaceful settlement issues (61.3 per cent). Similarly, prior to the group formation they divided on all issues to a certain degree, but since then they have divided only on peaceful settlement, human rights, and administrative, procedural, and structural issues (Charts 54 and 55). A similar increase in identical voting and a decrease in divided voting is evidenced in the votes on recommendations (Charts 56 and 57).

In terms of the over-all political phenomenon of causcusing group formation in the General Assembly, the voting of the majority of the Western European caucus in relation to the voting of the Assembly majority has very suggestive connotations (Chart 58). Since the VIIIth Session, when there were *ad hoc* consultations of the Brussels Treaty powers before the caucus was formally operating, these states have steadily increased the proportion of the votes in which they were in the Assembly majority. On the over-all basis of votes the majority voted with the Assembly majority 69.2 per cent of the time before and 79.8 per cent of the time after the group was formed. They were in opposition to the Assembly majority in 24.5 per cent of the votes before and 13.7 per cent after. On every subject except peaceful settlement issues the majority of the group was with the Assembly majority to a greater degree after the organization of the group than before (Charts 59 and 60). The decline in the peaceful settlement issues reflects the votes of the group with respect to the Suez situation and the French position vis-à-vis that situation. Charts 61 and 62 reflect the same trend in votes on recommendations involved.

It must be noted, of course, that our data on the Western European caucusing group is limited to only three sessions of the General Assembly.

THE AFRICAN CAUCUSING GROUP

The admission to the United Nations of Libya at the end of the Xth Session, Sudan, Morocco, and Tunisia at the start of the XIth Session, Ghana at the end of the XIth Session and Guinea at the XIIIth Session more than doubled the African members in the Assembly. Discussions on the possibilities of organizing an African caucusing group were first held among the representatives of these states who attended the Independence Celebration in Ghana. Subsequently, Ghana issued invitations to a Conference of African States in Accra and conducted preliminary negotiations prior to the conference. The object of the conference, which met in April 1958, was "to produce an African identity and personality in international affairs." [15] A Draft Memorandum on the Conference explained:

(5) The time has come for Africa to view the international situation in the light of her own interests. Where it suits her long-term interest to ally herself with particular countries in Europe, the Western Hemisphere and Asia, she might come to specific arrangements to safeguard her interests. In all other matters, it might be prudent and wise to decide her attitude to each issue as it arises in accordance with her interests, the interests of her friends and allies, her position in the comity of nations, and the interests of peace and justice. It is not proposed that the states of Africa should dissociate themselves from the Afro-Asian group of nations. It will, it can be expected, strengthen this group, however, if the African states have a definite and collective contribution to make to the deliberations of this group. . . .

. . . . .

(13) It is the hope . . . that the Conference will result in the setting up of a permanent machinery for cooperation and consultation among the states of Africa. This permanent organization may be concerned with:

. . . . .

(d) providing machinery for the prompt exchange of views on problems affecting Africa as a whole and on international problems so that the "mind" of Africa may be quickly mobilized, i.e., to ensure that an African "personality" in international affairs may become a reality. . . .

At the Conference agreement was reached on these points, and the African caucusing group began to operate in 3rd emergency special session and the XIIIth Session in the fall of 1958.

The Accra Conference indicated that questions of self-determination, racial equality, and economic development and collective measures for the reduction and control of armaments would be of primary concern to the members of the group; and in these areas of common concern there is reason to believe that they may reach a degree of effective unity. In other areas there is room for play for several potentially divisive factors. Ethiopia, Liberia, and Libya certainly have indicated a pro-Western attitude in the past, while Egypt and

[15] Ghana, "Draft Memorandum Conference of African States" (typewritten document, no date or symbol, author's files).

Syria, now the United Arab Republic, have been anti-West in orientation. Morocco and Tunisia have not been particularly friendly with the United Arab Republic. Ghana has a close relationship economically with Israel in opposition to the attitude of the United Arab Republic. In general, there is little common affinity in the sense of traditional relations amongst the group members, they are far from being in close geographical proximity, and do not necessarily have complementing economies. Their strongest common ties would seem to originate in the immediate fact that they are all newly independent and all moved both by surging nationalism and common bitter memories of previous Western domination.

An examination of the voting record of the members of the African caucusing group is suggestive, but, since there have been only three sessions in which most of them have been members of the United Nations, it hardly warrants conclusions. While the trends noted below are limited to the votes since the group was organized the charts also indicate the trends of the group in the Assembly before the group was formed.

On an over-all basis (Chart 63) the members of the group voted identically 45.5 per cent of the time and divided 9.0 per cent. It appears that they are likely to agree on issues involving peaceful settlement, economic, social, and humanitarian cooperation, and human rights (Chart 64) and on recommendations involving the supplying of funds and information (Chart 65). On an over-all basis the majority have been with the Assembly majority 51.5 per cent of the time and against the majority 24.6 per cent of the time (Chart 66) and with the Assembly majority to the greatest degree on matters involving human rights and economic cooperation (Chart 67). There appears to be little difference (Chart 68) as to the voting of the majority of these states with the Assembly majority according to the types of recommendations involved in the voting.

GEOGRAPHICAL DISTRIBUTION GROUPS

There is not much point in examining the voting record of the geographical distribution groups as such for clues to their cohesive and divisive elements. These groups exist primarily for the purpose of agreeing on nominations for elective posts, and those which have any strong sense of cohesion are identical with caucusing groups. The Asian and African geographical distribution group is identical with the Asian-African caucusing group; the Latin American geographical distribution group is identical with the Latin American caucusing group; and the Commonwealth geographical distribution group is identical with the Commonwealth caucusing group. With the exception of the addition of Finland and Yugoslavia, the Eastern European caucusing group is identical in membership with the Soviet caucusing group. In practice, of course, the combination of the Soviet bloc, the Latin American caucusing group and the Asian-African caucusing group has established the basis of the geographical distribution groups, a pattern which has recognized the special interests of the five permanent members of the Security Council but has placed all the other states in one geographical distribution category. Thus the states in the Western European geographical distribution group have been "lumped" together, so to speak, in a strange collection of members which it would not be very productive to examine.

REGIONAL GROUPS

Several of the regional groups are identical in membership with previously considered groups and blocs. Thus the Arab League corresponds to the Arab caucusing group, the Commonwealth is the same as the Commonwealth caucusing group, the Nordic Council is identical with the Scandinavian caucusing group, the Conference of African States is identical with the African group, and the Warsaw Pact corresponds to the Soviet bloc. To all intents, the Bandung Conference corresponds with the Asian-African group at one stage of its membership. The membership of the Western European caucus and that of the European Atomic Energy Community, the European Coal and Steel Community, and the European Common Market are identical.

We turn here to a brief examination of the others, with the exception of the Organization of the American States, considered later, to see what influence they have had in the Assembly and the extent to which their formation has affected the voting of their members. Since for the most part the regional groups as such have not had much effect on the nature of voting in the General Assembly and do not appear to play a significant over-all role in the bloc politics picture in the United Nations, our analysis is limited to significant resolution votes.[16]

The ANZUS Council, established in September 1951 by the United States, Australia, and New Zealand, seems to have had little effect on the voting of these states in the General Assembly. Prior to the establishment of this regional arrangement they voted identically 75.8 per cent of the time; they have voted identically 78.2 per cent of the time since. Prior to the agreement they divided 13.8 per cent; they have divided on 5.4 per cent of the votes since. If there has been any marked effect of the agreement it seems to have been to increase the frequency with which the members have abstained rather than vote against each other — assuming of course that this was the only factor affecting their votes. The votes of these countries show that prior to the regional grouping a majority of them voted with the Assembly majority 75.8 per cent of the time and since the agreement 73.0 per cent. Before the agreement a majority opposed the Assembly majority 17.2 per cent; since, 16.2 per cent. Thus there appears to have been little effective change in the voting patterns of this regional group as a result of the regional pact.

The Baghdad Pact establishing the Middle East Treaty Organization seems to have had some effect on voting patterns. Prior to the Pact, Iran, Iraq, Pakistan, Turkey, and the United Kingdom voted identically only 39.2 per cent of the time.[17] Since the Pact these countries have voted identically 55.0 per cent of the time. Similarly, prior to the Pact they divided on 26.2 per cent of the votes and since

[16] See p. 22 for an explanation of this type of vote sample. These votes do not include the voting in the XIIIth Session, but are based on the first 12 years of the Assembly.

[17] Iraq withdrew from the Baghdad Pact in 1959.

the Pact they have been divided only 15 per cent of the time. Since the Pact, agreement of the majority of these countries with the Assembly majority has increased from 80.5 per cent to 90 per cent. An analysis of the votes according to subjects shows that much of this increase of cohesion is traceable to agreement on matters related to collective measures and peaceful settlement. Generally, the United Kingdom is the member of this group that is most likely to be in opposition or abstention. Iraq of course is no longer a member.

The Balkan Alliance, composed of Greece, Turkey, and Yugoslavia, seems to have had little effect on voting in the General Assembly. Prior to the signing of the Alliance in December 1952, these three countries voted identically 31.6 per cent of the time; since, 32.2 per cent. There has been some tendency to increased abstentions rather than opposing each other; the divided votes have decreased from 31.6 per cent before to 17.8 per cent since the agreement. Although this may simply be the result of the alteration of Yugoslavia's position with respect to the Soviet bloc, one might be misled in dismissing the effect of this Alliance; an examination of the other "Western European" organizations to which Greece belongs, such as the North Atlantic Treaty Organization, shows that Greece is one of the states most likely to vote against the other members. The majority of the Balkan Alliance has voted with the Assembly majority on 76.3 per cent of the votes prior to the agreement and only 57.2 per cent of the votes since the agreement. The group majority has opposed the Assembly majority about 10.6 per cent of the time both before and since the agreement. These figures would seem to imply that, although the majority of this group does not now support the Assembly majority as much as previously, it tends to abstain rather than openly oppose.

The Council of Europe and the Organization for European Economic Cooperation have apparently had very little effect on the voting of members. Before the agreements these members voted identically 50 per cent to 52 per cent of the time; since, they have voted identically about 40 per cent to 45 per cent of the time. In fact, since the agreements, the degree of divided votes has risen from about 21 per cent to nearly 30 per cent. A similar result is evident in respect to the votes of the majority of these groups vis-à-vis the Assembly majority. Prior to the agreements the member states voted with the Assembly majority about 79 per cent of the time; since, about 74 per cent. Prior to the agreements they opposed the Assembly majority 5 per cent of the time; since, about 15 per cent. Part of the explanation of these votes may be in the fact that the membership of the Assembly has included an increasing number of the group members. It should be noted Greece and Sweden tend to deviate the most from the other members of the groups.

On an over-all basis the North Atlantic Treaty Organization seems to have had little effect on the votes of its members in the General Assembly. It is true that a trend may be observed on a session-by-session examination,[18] but it is probably explained by other factors than the cohesive elements of the NATO countries — for instance, shifting coalitions between caucusing groups in the Assembly. At any rate, prior to the NATO agreement in April 1949 the members voted identically 47.4 per cent of the time; since 1949 they have voted identically 55.4 per cent. Prior to the NATO agreement they divided on 21.1 per cent of the votes; since, they have divided on 21.3 per cent of the votes. There has been some change in the voting of the majority of the NATO regional group with the Assembly majority. Agreement of the group majority with the Assembly majority has decreased from 94.5 per cent to 76.5 per cent; and opposition to the Assembly majority has increased from 5.4 per cent to 14.9 per cent of the votes. It would seem that the group has succeeded in uniting coalitions of other groups in the Assembly against its position without developing sufficient real internal identity (i.e., only 55 per cent or so) to offset any united opposition. In the sense that within the NATO membership there exists the bulk of the Benelux, Western European, and Scandinavian caucusing groups, the NATO regional group is divided into factions. Greece, Norway, and Denmark appear to deviate most within the NATO group.

[18] See Waldo Chamberlin, "The North Atlantic Bloc in the UN General Assembly," *Orbis 1* (1958), 459–473.

The creation of the Organization of the Central American States in October 1951 seems to have had a cohesive effect on the five members. Although divided votes have increased from 24.2 per cent to 29.8 per cent, identical voting has increased from 48.3 per cent to 67.5 per cent of the votes. The increase in identical voting is reflected in an increase of agreement with the Assembly majority from 56.3 per cent to 96.6 per cent and a decrease in opposition to the Assembly majority from 13.8 per cent to 0.0 per cent. This latter development has to be related to the fact that this group is a unit within the Latin American caucus, which is generally with the Assembly majority. Guatemala is the member of this group most likely to deviate or abstain.

The creation of the South East Asian Treaty Organization prior to the Xth Session seems to have affected the voting of these members, particularly the Asian members of the group. Identical voting has increased from 37.0 per cent to 75.0 per cent; divided voting has decreased from 34.8 per cent to 10 per cent of the votes. Likewise, there has been an increase in the group's agreement with the Assembly majority from 76.1 per cent to 90 per cent and a decrease in opposition from 17.4 per cent to 5 per cent. These figures may be misleading unless one remembers that they relate to the votes of the majority of the group. The three Asian members of this group — Pakistan, Thailand, and the Philippines — may oppose the Assembly majority, but, if the five other members of the group agree, the group majority will still be with the Assembly majority. Thus far the three Asian states have been more in agreement with the other members of the group since the SEATO agreement, and are referred to as pro-Western members of the Asian-African Caucus.

Lastly, a look at the members of the Western European Union (formerly the Brussels Treaty Organization) indicates that their voting habits have been similar to those of the NATO group. Since the Western European Union came into being shortly after the United Nations itself began, there are too few votes "before" to make a before-and-after comparison valid. On the over-all basis the members of WEU vote identically 75.0 per cent and are divided 3.6

per cent of the time. The majority of the WEU members vote with the Assembly majority on 76.8 per cent and oppose the majority of the Assembly on 17.9 per cent of the votes.

In all of these regional groups the highest degree of cohesion is on votes connected with collective measures and peaceful settlement issues.

COMMON INTEREST GROUPS

Since the common interest groups are usually coalitions of caucusing groups, most of them will be considered in the next section. Three common interest groups are briefly considered here on the basis of an analysis of significant resolution votes.

On an over-all basis, the Moslem common interest group has voted identically only 43.9 per cent of the time, yet it has divided on only 13.7 per cent of the votes. Turkey is the member most likely to deviate from the group. The majority of this group has voted with the Assembly majority on 60.6 per cent and disagreed on 15.1 per cent of the votes.

The so-called Big Three — France, United Kingdom, and the United States — are often considered as a common interest group. They have voted identically on 72.6 per cent and divided on 6.1 per cent of the votes. Division has been generally on issues relating to self-determination and, in some instances, peaceful settlement matters such as the Suez situation in 1956. A majority of these three have voted with the Assembly majority 70.1 per cent and opposed the Assembly majority 15.2 per cent of the time.

Lastly, a brief look at the common interest group made up of the trust territory administrators shows that the members have voted identically on 65.2 per cent and divided on 13.7 per cent of the votes, and that the majority of this group has voted with the majority of the Assembly 72.7 per cent and against the Assembly majority 16.7 per cent of the votes.

IV   BLOC AND GROUP COALITIONS

The preceding discussion of the make-up and voting records of individual groups in the General Assembly furnishes one set of dimensions, so to speak, of the extensiveness of bloc politics in the United Nations. To complete the picture, to give depth to its implications, it is necessary to consider the relations between organized groups. Without attempting the wearisome, if not impossible, task of identifying every coalition of blocs and groups that has been formed over the twelve-year history of the United Nations, we can, by examining generally the interrelations between blocs and groups, get some indications as to which of them are most likely to come together in a given situation.

RELATIONSHIP OF GROUPS TO THE ASSEMBLY MAJORITY

On an over-all basis (Chart 69) the groups might be ranked by the percentage by which they are in accord with the Assembly majority as follows: [1]

Latin American	87.6	Benelux	69.9
Western European	79.8	Scandinavian	68.7
U.S.A.	75.6	Arab	66.6
Commonwealth	75.0	African	51.5
Asian-African	70.1	Soviet	39.4

This ranking would suggest that, according to the vote of their majorities, the Latin American, Western European, and Common-

---

[1] For the purpose of this chart and the subsequent figures in this section the votes of each of the blocs and groups are based only on the period for which they existed as organized caucusing groups. In the case of the African group, which did not operate until the XIIIth Session, the generalizations should be very cautiously evaluated because they do not really include enough votes for a fair sample of the trends of this group.

wealth groups tend to dominate voting in the Assembly and that the
Soviet bloc is always in the minority role. When we take into ac-
count the fact that there have been fluctuations from session to session, and list the votes by session, we see that such conclusions are
somewhat oversimplified (Chart 70).

Majority Votes by General Assembly Session

(percentages based on an adjusted gross number of roll-call votes)

I(1) — 1946:

Latin America	100	Arab	58.4
Benelux	100	Scandinavian	50.0
Commonwealth	91.7	Soviet	33.3
U.S.A.	75.0		

I(2) — 1946:

Latin America	100	U.S.A.	78.1
Scandinavian	87.0	Arab	69.6
Commonwealth	82.5	Soviet	30.5
Benelux	78.4		

II — 1947:

Latin America	87.5	Benelux	79.1
U.S.A.	87.5	Arab	54.4
Scandinavian	83.2	Soviet	37.5
Commonwealth	79.2		

III — 1948:

U.S.A.	84.4	Scandinavian	77.1
Latin America	81.8	Arab	60.2
Commonwealth	80.6	Soviet	26.5
Benelux	79.5		

IV — 1949:

Latin America	83.0	Soviet	59.5
Arab	76.6	U.S.A.	55.3
Benelux	70.3	Scandinavian	40.2
Commonwealth	65.8		

V — 1950:

Latin America	95.3	Scandinavian	69.0
U.S.A.	90.5	Benelux	61.9
Arab	88.5	Commonwealth	61.8
Asian-African	80.7	Soviet	30.3

VI — 1951:

Latin America	91.0	Scandinavian	50.0
Arab	77.4	U.S.A.	50.0
Asian-African	77.3	Benelux	40.9
Soviet	50.2	Commonwealth	36.5

VII — 1952:

Latin America	87.2	Scandinavian	63.4
Arab	70.8	Benelux	58.6
Asian-African	68.3	Commonwealth	56.1
U.S.A.	65.7	Soviet	39.0

VIII — 1953:

Latin America	91.7	U.S.A.	58.4
Arab	75.0	Soviet	58.3
Asian-African	66.6	Commonwealth	54.2
Scandinavian	62.5	Benelux	41.7

IX — 1954:

Asian-African	84.9	Benelux	60.7
Arab	82.1	Scandinavian	60.7
Latin America	68.6	U.S.A.	57.2
Commonwealth	60.8	Soviet	39.3

X — 1955:

Asian-African	84.9	Arab	66.6
Latin America	84.9	U.S.A.	66.6
Commonwealth	81.6	Scandinavian	63.7
Benelux	72.7	Soviet	63.5

XI — 1956:

Latin America	91.0	Benelux	75.0
Commonwealth	90.9	Asian-African	72.5
U.S.A.	88.5	Arab	51.2
Scandinavian	84.0	Soviet	39.5
Western European	75.0		

XII — 1957:

Latin America	96.8	Scandinavian	74.2
Commonwealth	93.6	Asian-African	64.5
U.S.A.	81.1	Arab	50.0
Benelux	77.5	Soviet	34.5
Western European	77.2		

XIII — 1958:

Commonwealth	100.0	Scandinavian	63.5
Latin America	91.0	Asian-African	60.7
U.S.A.	87.9	African	51.1
Western European	72.6	Arab	48.6
Benelux	69.5	Soviet	42.4

Several trends are apparent in the sessional fluctuations of the caucusing groups which have dominated the Assembly voting. Early domination by the Latin American group in conjunction with the Commonwealth, Benelux, and Scandinavian groups was gradually altered as first the Arab group and then the Asian-African group joined Latin America in leading the majority. With continuing division in the so-called "Western" groups, the Asian-African and Arab groups led the majority in the IXth Session. By the Xth Session, the Latin American group and the Commonwealth group regained their earlier position, and in the last two sessions the "Western Groups" were once again "in control" of the Assembly majority. The voting of the United States with the majority has followed approximately the trend of the other "Western" groups, although it has on occasion fluctuated more markedly. Although all of these percentages have been figured to include the requirement for either a simple majority or a two-thirds majority, whichever was necessary, a detailed examination of the votes suggests that "Western" groups are being required to modify their initial proposals to a greater degree in order to build a two-thirds majority. For the most part, the Soviet Union has retained its minority role, although Chart 70 demonstrates an extraordinary cyclical rise and fall pattern of voting. In part this appears a reflection of the types of issues which dominated and characterize each session. The IIId Session, for example,

is often called the "human rights" session. The Soviet pattern also reflects, to a degree, the cyclical shifts in the approaches of Soviet
policy since 1945.

GROUP RELATIONS TO THE ASSEMBLY MAJORITY ACCORDING TO CATEGORIES OF ISSUES

While the record of over-all voting furnishes many insights into
the general nature of the coalitions which have decided voting in
the Assembly in the various sessions, it is also pertinent to look at
the voting according to subjects in order to see which groups tend
to constitute the Assembly majority in specific situations. In considering this analysis reservations have to be kept constantly in
mind in evaluating the percentages of the African and Western
European groups because they have only been in existence a comparatively short time and are as a result based on a much smaller
number of votes than the other groups.

Collective measures. On the votes concerned with collective measures and such issues as the regulation of armaments the caucusing
groups can be arranged in the following order according to the
degree to which they have been with the Assembly majority on
these issues: [2]

Western European	100.0	Arab	76.4
Latin American	98.1	Commonwealth	73.8
U.S.A.	96.0	Benelux	71.5
Scandinavian	80.0	African	66.6
Asian-African	79.5	Soviet	15.9

Here again the Soviet Union has obviously been in opposition to the
Assembly majority. The position of the Benelux group is surprising,
although in part explained by opposition to votes in the Suez situation in 1956. The Western European group does not reflect these
Suez votes because the group was not operating at that time. The

[2] These and other rank lists do not imply that the members of the group
voted identically; these are the percentages by which the majority of the group
supported the vote of the Assembly majority.

groups abstain on issues involving collective measures to the following degree:

Arab	19.7	Benelux	6.5
Commonwealth	16.2	U.S.A.	2.1
Scandinavian	16.0	Latin American	1.9
Soviet	15.7	African	0.0
Asian-African	12.8	Western European	0.0

Peaceful settlement. On peaceful settlement issues the caucusing groups support the Assembly majority in the following order:

Latin American	92.9	Scandinavian	63.5
Benelux	75.5	Asian-African	62.5
Commonwealth	72.6	Western European	55.7
U.S.A.	72.0	Soviet	39.4
Arab	67.6	African	33.3

The fact that most of the groups voted between 65 per cent and 75 per cent of the time with the majority would seem to imply that the coalitions on these issues are fairly flexible, with no hard and fast coalition at the top. The degree to which the groups abstain on peaceful settlement issues is as follows:

African	33.3	Soviet	11.2
Asian-African	32.8	Commonwealth	9.2
Western European	22.1	U.S.A.	9.1
Arab	20.3	Benelux	6.3
Scandinavian	13.0	Latin American	5.1

The high degree of abstentions by the Asian-African Group certainly is indicative of the "neutralist" tendencies of the group and is in considerable contrast to the record of the Latin American group, which appears to take a strong positive role on most issues.

Self-determination. The relationships of the groups on self-determination matters indicate that there has been continuing vying for leadership in these matters. Support has been as follows:

Western European	78.6	Scandinavian	71.1
Latin American	75.0	U.S.A.	70.4

Commonwealth	68.5	Asian-African	59.2
Benelux	64.0	Soviet	44.6
Arab	60.6	African	25.0

The coalitions seem to be of two kinds depending upon the nature of the self-determination issues. On broad principles of self-determination, the Latin American, Asian-African, Arab, and sometimes Soviet groups are allied. On self-determination issues involving particular problems, such as Tunisia, the Latin American group generally is allied with the "Western" groups. The record of abstention on self-determination matters by the groups is:

African	75.0	Latin American	6.9
Asian-African	26.7	Commonwealth	6.0
Arab	14.5	Benelux	5.8
Soviet	9.5	Scandinavian	5.4
U.S.A.	8.4	Western European	0.0

One reason for the high degree of abstentions by the Asian-African group may be the fact that the group is divided internally on specific application issues of self-determination. The comparatively small degree of abstentions by the "Western" groups indicates that these groups tend to take strong positions on questions of self-determination.

Economic, social, and humanitarian. Analyzing the votes on economic, social, and humanitarian cooperation ranks the groups in the following order according to the degree to which they support the majority position:

African	100.0	Scandinavian	75.7
Latin American	92.6	Benelux	70.7
U.S.A.	80.5	Arab	62.2
Commonwealth	80.5	Asian-African	58.4
Western European	81.8	Soviet	32.5

This ranking definitely indicates that the Arab, Asian-African, and Soviet groups are in the minority generally, the coalitions here being formed of other groups. Abstentions on these issues are as follows:

Asian-African	29.1	Commonwealth	4.9
Benelux	17.1	Soviet	4.6
Arab	13.0	Latin American	0.0
Scandinavian	9.6	Western European	0.0
U.S.A.	7.3	African	0.0

Human rights. A somewhat different coalition ranking is evident on matters involving human rights. The order in which the groups support the majority is as follows:

Latin American	94.6	Commonwealth	66.0
Arab	73.7	Soviet	54.4
U.S.A.	73.2	Benelux	50.0
Scandinavian	73.1	Western European	50.0
Asian-African	70.0	African	50.0

The Benelux, Western European, and Commonwealth groups, as well as the Soviet bloc, are generally in a minority position on human rights according to the voting record. However, with the exception of the Latin American group, none is overwhelmingly with the majority; and the degree of abstentions by most groups indicates that the positions are not hard and fast on human rights issues.

Western European	25.0	Scandinavian	12.6
Arab	19.3	Benelux	10.7
U.S.A.	17.9	Commonwealth	7.2
Asian-African	17.5	Soviet	7.0
African	14.0	Latin American	1.8

Development of international law. The groups most likely to be in the majority on issues relating to the development of international law might be inferred from the following indication of the degree to which the groups have supported the majority position on these issues.

Western European	100.0	U.S.A.	69.6
African	100.0	Arab	65.4
Latin American	93.7	Benelux	63.5
Asian-African	81.8	Scandinavian	57.6
Commonwealth	78.7	Soviet	38.0

The Western European group and the Soviet bloc are definitely in a minority position. The Latin American, Asian-African, and Commonwealth groups appear to be in agreement most on issues relating to the development of international law. The extent of abstentions is as follows:

Soviet	10.4	Benelux	6.3
Arab	10.2	Latin American	0.3
Asian-African	10.1	Commonwealth	0.0
U.S.A.	9.1	African	0.0
Scandinavian	9.1	Western European	0.0

The lack of abstentions by the Commonwealth group indicates that this group takes a definite stand on these issues.

Administration, procedure, and structure. With respect to issues involving administration, procedure, and structure, the groups vote with the majority in the following order:

Latin American	90.7	Benelux	77.1
Commonwealth	83.3	Arab	70.5
U.S.A.	79.9	Scandinavian	69.2
Western European	79.5	Soviet	41.0
Asian-African	78.1	African	27.2

The groups abstain on these procedural matters in the following order:

African	18.3	U.S.A.	8.3
Western European	14.4	Benelux	8.2
Arab	10.9	Asian-African	7.5
Soviet	10.4	Commonwealth	4.5
Scandinavian	8.7	Latin American	1.9

Some interesting conclusions are suggested by these ranking lists. In the first place, it is fairly obvious that the Latin American group is with the majority regardless of subject. Considering the degree to which this group does not vote identically within its membership, the dominant role of the group is remarkable, indicating, as was suggested earlier, a notable ability to adjust and modify its position so as to keep in a variety of coalitions. On the other hand, it is apparent that the groups which have a very cohesive internal voting record, such as the Soviet bloc and the Arab, Benelux, and Scandinavian groups, generally tend toward a minority position, their very cohesion perhaps preventing them from making the adjustments in their policy manipulations which would allow them to join in the majority view.

With the possible exception of votes on economic, social, and humanitarian cooperation, the United States seems to have pursued a course of action which has kept it with the majority of the Assembly to a fairly high degree. Regardless of the subject, the Soviet bloc has been in a minority role — but not always alone. Contrary to the feeling of many observers, the Asian-African group is not opposed by the other groups to the extent that it is in a minority position. Quite the contrary, the Asian-African group, percentage-wise, is in a fairly high coalition position.

V SOME POLICY IMPLICATIONS

When we turn from the dissection of bloc politics in the
United Nations — from the formation, nature, and voting records of
the individual blocs and groups of member states — to the implications of the total phenomenon, it seems premature to attempt any
set of formal conclusions. At this stage in the history of the various
groupings — some new, some well established, large and small —
the student of international organization will prefer to engage in
any such effort for himself. It may, however, be appropriate to set
down some observations reflecting not the conclusive substance but
the general direction of certain lines of reasoning which appear
logical in the context of the history outlined in the foregoing discussion.

It may be argued that, as the United Nations has become enlarged
both in its membership and in terms of the variety of interests represented in that membership, the bloc and group arrangements have
become a necessity for effective negotiation. In any case, it is clear
that participation in a caucusing group is advantageous to a member
state, and participation in several caucus groups even more advantageous. It provides an opportunity to create a combined voting
power which can be a critical factor in negotiating with other
groups. A state which does not belong to a caucusing group is forced
to rely upon more subtle political and economic pressures for gain-
ing support for its point of view and consequently must risk individual moves which may have lasting unfavorable effects. Participation
in caucusing groups can open avenues for a variety of diplomatic
techniques. A group caucus pursuing a common point of view can
cast its members in different roles in order to explore possible areas
of negotiation. A group caucus can benefit from collective interpre-
tations of factors present in other groups, a procedure which can

often indicate subtleties of cohesion and division that are pertinent to working out acceptable compromises. Participation in a caucusing group itself indicates a willingness to seek areas of acceptable compromise, whereas failure to participate in caucusing groups can suggest an intransigent attitude which is hardly conducive to successful diplomacy.

On the other hand, bloc politics is not an unmixed blessing. It creates a potential for manipulative dealing in votes to the detriment of the United Nations as a whole and to the development of peace; and it led, in fact, in the earlier sessions to a definite trend towards what Sir Carl Berendsen called an "irresponsible bargaining" of votes. Although there is no acute present danger of such a development, there is no sure protection against it until a more realistic voting arrangement is adopted for the General Assembly. Actually it is improper to charge "irresponsible bargaining" if a delegate is pursuing instructions from his Foreign Office. It may have been that in the earlier sessions most delegates had fewer specific instructions than now appears evident. One often hears in the United Nations corridors that positions are run by the Foreign Offices "now." If delegates are carefully pursuing their instructions they can hardly be accused of not being responsible, and it has to be recognized that changing the voting arrangements, if such were possible, will not of itself alter the policies pursued by the various Foreign Offices. Lastly it might be argued that another disadvantage of bloc politics is its inflexibility. This judgment remains to be proven. Within each group there are many divisive elements which are factors in stimulating flexibility. The formation of the African group within the Asian-African group may be a trend in this direction and events in the resumed XIIIth Session between these groups suggest that such a possibility may develop. Certainly there is an opportunity for encouraging factors influencing flexibility by delegations so concerned.

At the present stage of its development, bloc politics in the United Nations has two particular features which invite speculation. In the first place, caucusing groups and blocs are to a considerable extent regional in character, which suggests that contacts and negotiations on a regional basis are fairly easily carried over into the United Nations, formalizing what is a natural procedure which then can be carried out from both ends, so to speak. A committee of delegates in the African caucusing group toured the Latin American capitals to consult on issues pending before the XIIIth Session of the Assembly. For several years certain members of the Asian-African group have been designated to carry on negotiations in Latin American foreign offices at the same time that the caucus in the Assembly was negotiating with the Latin American United Nations representatives. Secondly, at the moment, the individual blocs and groups appear to be primarily concerned with only a limited range of issues. The Asian-African caucusing group, for instance, seems to be most closely united on matters relating to economic development and self-determination of peoples. This combination takes on considerable interest when one tries to look ahead.

It seems probable that, as the United Nations reaches near-universality, the number of regionally oriented caucusing groups is likely to increase, and that, as they mature, the individual groups will both develop increasing internal rapport and broaden the range of issues on which they can unite in the General Assembly. These apparently natural developments do not appear very encouraging when one is reminded that when issues in debate are framed in regional terms they usually become oversimplified as questions of principle — of developed versus underdeveloped countries, East versus West, colonial versus anti-colonial. Once such broad principles are emphasized, the regionally oriented caucusing groups are forced to choose sides, and the area for negotiation is narrowed almost to the point where it is impossible to remove issues of contention. One has only to note, for example, that, if the United States, in its concern for Western European unity against the Soviet threat, carries its support for the European powers to the extent of refusing to support self-determination interests of Asian and African states, such action can only solidify the Asian-African caucus against all United States attitudes. As the United Nations approaches universal membership of the world community of states, and if present trends continue, there is a very real possibility that group coalitions may prevent conclusive decisions by the organization.

It goes without saying that, whatever its immediate advantages to individual member states, bloc and group development can make a constructive contribution to negotiation within the United Nations only so long as it does not become stabilized in the form of large intransigent groups. In the interest of every member nation of the United Nations as well as in the interest of the United Nations as a whole, it would seem essential to encourage the development of smaller rather than larger caucusing groups. And it would seem that, if the General Assembly is not to be reduced to a battle of opposites which results in watered-down platitudes in the form of resolutions, encouragement will have to be given to developing interest bases rather than regional bases for caucusing groups. If negotiation both within and outside of the United Nations structure were concerned with encouraging smaller caucusing groups based upon like interests in particular areas, the maneuverability of members would be greatly increased. If the breadth of possible coalitions were increased through the existence of smaller caucusing groups, issues might tend to be resolved more often on a basis relevant to the issue than on the basis of broad principles. It may be argued size in itself is not significant and one would have to agree. The objection to large groups is intended as an objection to groups so large comparatively that they represent not regionalism, which might be useful, but they represent what some might call "unholy" combinations which are more successful in opposition than in pressing for viable solutions to issues. If efforts were directed to creating groups so small that they had no cohesion except on a particular issue, there is a danger the Assembly might become frustrated by fractionization.

Efforts to encourage smaller or more realistic regional caucusing groups will depend to a great extent upon the delegates' parliamentary sophistication. Since the resolution of peace is not so much dependent upon grandiose plays to the press and home audiences as on developing more and more areas of negotiation, success in the bloc and group structure of the United Nations should be measured not so much by the number of forced "vote victories" as by its effectiveness in maintaining further basis for discussion which prevents the crystallization of issues into oversimplified principles. Some importance, then, is attached to the presence in the United Nations of such men as Ali Sastroamidjojo, who has had the repeated experience of maintaining domestic political coalitions, or Paul-Henri Spaak, who has been a domestic parliamentary leader for a long period of time. Such men are more at home in the group structure of the United Nations than the career foreign service officer who has never been involved in domestic politics, where dealing with political pressure groups demands a wide variety of political skills. Obviously this is not to argue that all politicians are good, and all career foreign service officers are bad in Assembly negotiations; rather it is a plea for recognizing the necessity for parliamentary *savoir-faire*. Careful and extended observation of the negotiating process at the United Nations provides a wealth of evidence as to the success of delegates who have a fine appreciation of parliamentary sophistication.

Admittedly the General Assembly is not a legislative body in the sense that domestic parliaments are; yet the manner in which issues are negotiated and conclusions are reached is comparable with the national legislative process. National legislators do not arrive at major decisions on the floor of the legislative body but in behind-the-scenes negotiations, where informal interest factions impose their point of view on a complex of issues rather than on individual questions, and an effort is made to adjust positions on issues not of primary concern in order to obtain support on the more vital concerns from the other interest factions. The process is a continuous one in which a rapport with "opponents" is developed, so that a frank exchange of positions is always possible; and it is one in which the research and administrative assistants of the legislators also participate.

A sense of purpose, while recognizing the necessity for appealing to an electorate, also recognizes both the extent to which public appeals represent hard and fast positions and the extent to which a public statement is subject to a realistic modification. A sense of rapport leads to the possibility of breaking down the barriers of personality, making it possible to determine the differences between personal quirks and policy positions. It encourages frank exchanges which can often nurture public policy adjustments.

It is true that such influences on "opposing" positions have only gradual effect, and that some positions are not subject to modification. Nevertheless, a well developed rapport creates predictable confidence, and the extent of give-and-take rapport built up among members in domestic legislative bodies often relegates the steadfast members into a continual minority position. At the same time, the collegiate sense of a frank relationship with other members builds a strong and viable majority relationship that can persist and easily adjust to minor differences.

If such a sense of political maturity were consciously encouraged within the United Nations, the possibility of developing a coalescing majority would be greatly enhanced. Such a practice of parliamentary sophistication would gradually force the irreconcilable members into a cloistered minority. In a sense, then, negotiating in the bloc and group structure of the United Nations calls for less formalized procedures in which there is a constant association of members of delegations on all levels, not simply the ambassadorial level. Diplomatic techniques in such a setting call for more quiet and frank conversations, based on personalities and information acquired through all levels of personal contact which suggest the areas in which adjustments are possible.

It is a hopeful sign that the trend towards this sort of parliamentary sophistication is already developing, and that the members who are not sharing in its development are increasingly finding themselves in the position of exerting outside pressures to obtain support for their positions. Such support is not really friendly support and has to be constantly bolstered by further political and economic threats. It is already evident that success in the General Assembly depends not so much on a careful use of rules of procedures as it does upon using formalized procedure only to the extent that it does not hinder negotiation.

If the foregoing line of reasoning is correct, it is relevant here to note some impressions of the practices of the United States delegation in the United Nations.

The close observer of the bloc and group development is repeatedly confronted with the apparent inability of the United States to perceive its true nature and the consequent adjustments of the United States approach that are necessary to operate in such an atmosphere. Whether the charges are valid or not, one finds that members of other delegations frequently remark that their only contacts with the United States delegation are on a formal rather than informal basis, and that they can meet on a negotiating basis only with the Chief of the United States delegation. This charge against the United States is made to a greater degree by delegations whose governments are not as closely allied with the United States as certain other delegations. There is a feeling that the United States is not willing to be frank in confidential relations, a feeling that inspires growing distrust of the motives and intentions of the United States.

However inaccurate these impressions may be, the extent to which they prevail — even among the members of pro-United States delegations — cannot be ignored. One is almost shocked by the number of times which members of delegations desirous of understanding the United States position comment on the virtual lack of personal relations encouraged by the United States delegation on any level other than the ambassadorial level, where it is felt that the public policy position predominates.

It follows that, although there may be no good reason for skepticism about a given American position, since there is an inherent trend within the bloc and group relations to develop close and continuing personal contacts on all levels, the feeling that the United States will not participate has the effect of forcing the United States into a minority position. Members of other delegations, while recognizing that its position at the moment is not a minority one, insist that the United States commands the majority only by political and economic pressure and not by developing trust and understanding.

One is forced to consider with some misgivings the future role of the United States in the United Nations. Virtually all the members of the many delegations who express their concern mention what they call the "failures" of the United States with reluctance. Most of them are basically sympathetic to the United States. And yet the sense of distrust, or at least doubt, appears to be increasing as the various delegations develop increasing degrees of rapport and intimate contacts with other delegations, the members of which recognize the alteration of diplomatic negotiation techniques which are demanded in the bloc and group structure of the United Nations.

However, all of the preceding discussion on the role of the United States is not meant to imply that the United States has not been successful in its negotiations in the United Nations. As the voting records demonstrate, the United States has a surprisingly successful record in combining majorities. But in many instances this was accomplished by considerable pressure which may not be as successful in the future as the increases in membership alter the character of the Assembly and reduce the number of delegations closely allied with the United States. If the preceding criticisms are extreme, the intent is to pinpoint danger signs which may affect the United States position in the General Assembly in the future.

Bloc politics in the General Assembly can no longer be viewed as a temporary phenomenon. Blocs and groups now constitute a regularized, though informal, aspect of the organization of the United Nations; and there is every reason to believe that with the present voting arrangements they will play an increasing role. Thus each member must evaluate its policies and role in the United Nations with full awareness of the implications of the nature and extent of the bloc and group development.

Although present factors stress the regional character of the groups, they are all characterized by inherent elements of cohesion and division which can be nurtured as policy demands may require.

Any utilization of these inherent elements depends upon a "quiet" diplomatic technique. This is to argue that the future of the United Nations and the purpose of peace can be fostered to a greater degree by the development of a multiplicity of cross interests, none of which are exclusive, than by encouraging the present tendency toward positions based on exclusive and oversimplified principles which reduce the possibility of alternatives. Properly approached and developed, the bloc and group structure of the United Nations can substantially contribute towards political resolution of conflicting interests in the same way that such informal groups facilitate negotiations in domestic parliaments.

CHARTS 1–70

CHART 1   123

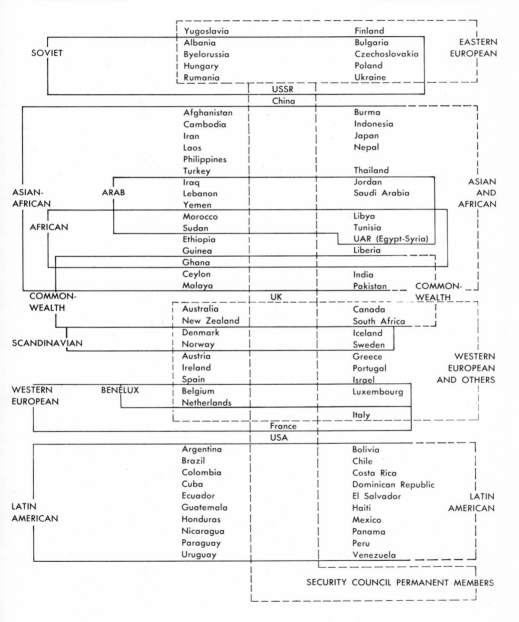

CAUCUSING GROUPS

GEOGRAPHICAL
DISTRIBUTION GROUPS

CAUCUSING GROUPS		GEOGRAPHICAL DISTRIBUTION GROUPS

SOVIET

Yugoslavia	Finland
Albania	Bulgaria
Byelorussia	Czechoslovakia
Hungary	Poland
Rumania	Ukraine

EASTERN
EUROPEAN

USSR
China

ASIAN-
AFRICAN   ARAB

Afghanistan	Burma
Cambodia	Indonesia
Iran	Japan
Laos	Nepal
Philippines	
Turkey	Thailand
Iraq	Jordan
Lebanon	Saudi Arabia
Yemen	

ASIAN
AND
AFRICAN

AFRICAN

Morocco	Libya
Sudan	Tunisia
Ethiopia	UAR (Egypt-Syria)
Guinea	Liberia
Ghana	
Ceylon	India
Malaya	Pakistan

COMMON-
WEALTH

COMMON-
WEALTH

UK

Australia	Canada
New Zealand	South Africa
Denmark	Iceland
Norway	Sweden
Austria	Greece
Ireland	Portugal
Spain	Israel
Belgium	Luxembourg
Netherlands	
	Italy

SCANDINAVIAN

WESTERN
EUROPEAN   BENELUX

WESTERN
EUROPEAN
AND OTHERS

France
USA

LATIN
AMERICAN

Argentina	Bolivia
Brazil	Chile
Colombia	Costa Rica
Cuba	Dominican Republic
Ecuador	El Salvador
Guatemala	Haiti
Honduras	Mexico
Nicaragua	Panama
Paraguay	Peru
Uruguay	Venezuela

LATIN
AMERICAN

SECURITY COUNCIL PERMANENT MEMBERS

1. Members of the United Nations arranged according to their membership in caucusing and geographical distribution groups operating in the General Assembly at the start of the XIVth Session in 1959

REGIONAL GROUPS

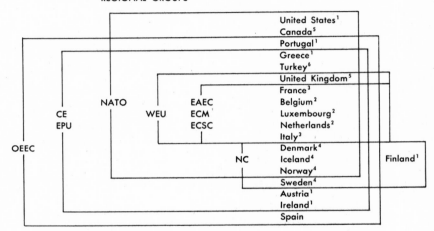

Symbol key to regional groups:
CE: Council of Europe
EAEC: European Atomic Energy Community
ECM: European Common Market
ECSC: European Coal and Steel Community
EPU: European Payments Union
NATO: North Atlantic Treaty Organization
NC: Nordic Council
OEEC: Organization for European Economic Cooperation
WEU: Western European Union (formerly Brussels Treaty Organization)

1. Does not belong to a caucusing group
2. Belongs to Benelux and Western European caucusing groups
3. Belongs to Western European caucusing group
4. Belongs to Scandinavian caucusing group
5. Belongs to Commonwealth caucusing group
6. Belongs to Asian-African caucusing group

2. Comparison of the membership in "Western European" regional groups and the membership in caucusing groups

CHART 3   125

MEMBERSHIP IN
CAUCUSING GROUPS

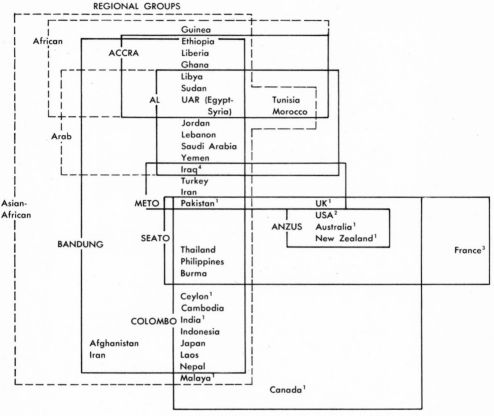

Symbol key to regional groups:
        ACCRA: Conference of Independent African States
        AL: Arab League
        ANZUS: Anzus Council
        BANDUNG: Asian-African Conference
        COLOMBO: Colombo Plan
        METO: Baghdad Pact
        SEATO: Southeast Asian Treaty Organization

1. Member of the Commonwealth caucusing group
2. Does not belong to a caucusing group
3. Member of Western European caucusing group
4. Member of Baghdad Pact until 1959

3. Comparison of the membership in "Asian and African" regional groups and the membership in caucusing groups, at the end of the XIIIth Session

REGIONAL GROUPS   MEMBERSHIP IN CAUCUSING GROUPS

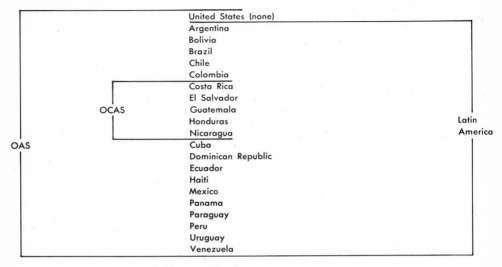

Symbol key to regional groups:
OAS: Organization of American States
OCAS: Organization of Central American States

4. Comparison of the membership in "American" regional groups and the membership in caucusing groups

REGIONAL GROUPS   MEMBERSHIP IN CAUCUSING GROUPS

5. Comparison of the membership in "Eastern European" regional groups and the membership in caucusing groups

CHART 6

127

CAUCUSING GROUPS

COMMON INTEREST GROUPS

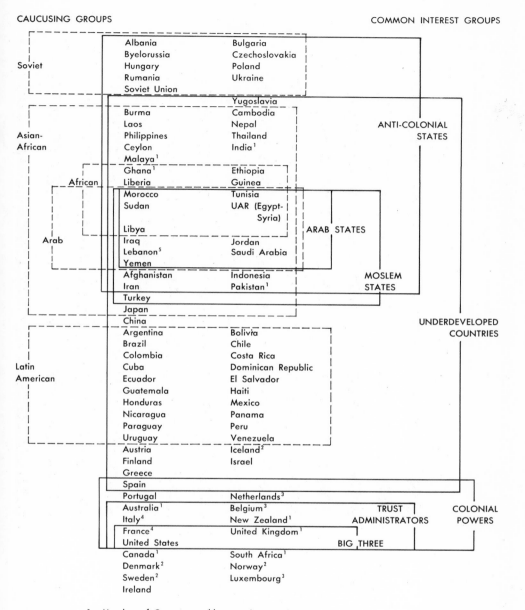

1. Member of Commonwealth caucusing group
2. Member of Scandinavian caucusing group
3. Member of both the Benelux and Western European caucusing groups
4. Member of Western European caucusing group
5. Lebanon might not be considered a "Moslem" state because the population is about equally divided between Moslems and Christians, with a slight Christian majority.

6. Comparison of membership in common interest groups and caucusing groups

CHART 7

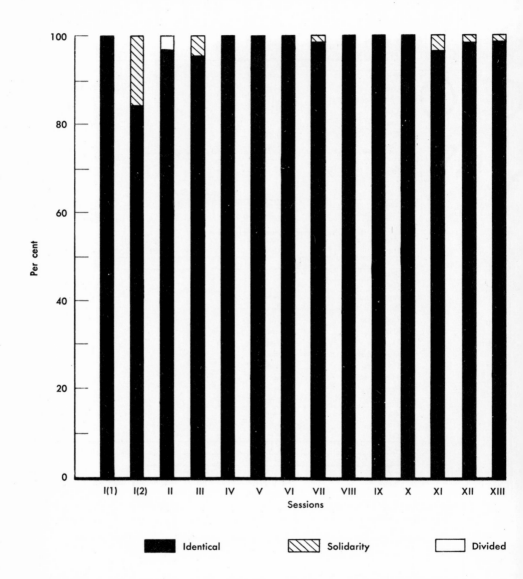

7. Cohesion of the Soviet bloc as evidenced by the types of votes (by per cent of the adjusted gross number of roll-call votes per regular session of the General Assembly)

CHART 8   129

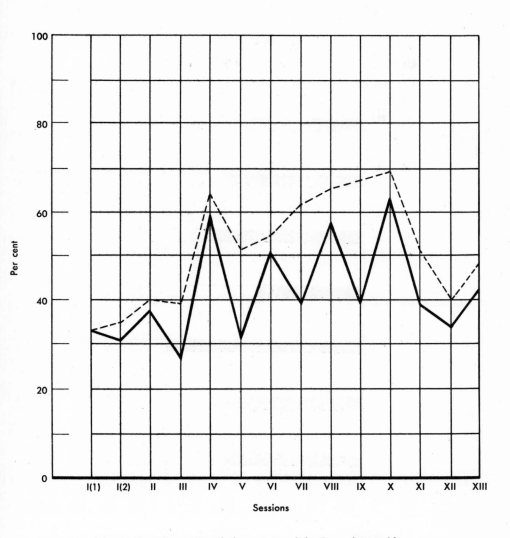

Per cent

Sessions

———— Per cent "in agreement" with the majority of the General Assembly
— — — Per cent "in agreement" plus per cent "not against" the majority of the General Assembly

Note: **The difference** between the two lines equals the per cent "not against."

8. Voting of the Soviet bloc in relation to the voting of the majority of the members of the General Assembly. (Vote of the majority of the Soviet bloc according to the per cent "in agreement" and the per cent "not against" the majority of the members of the General Assembly, based on an adjusted gross number of roll-call votes per regular session of the General Assembly.)

CHART 9

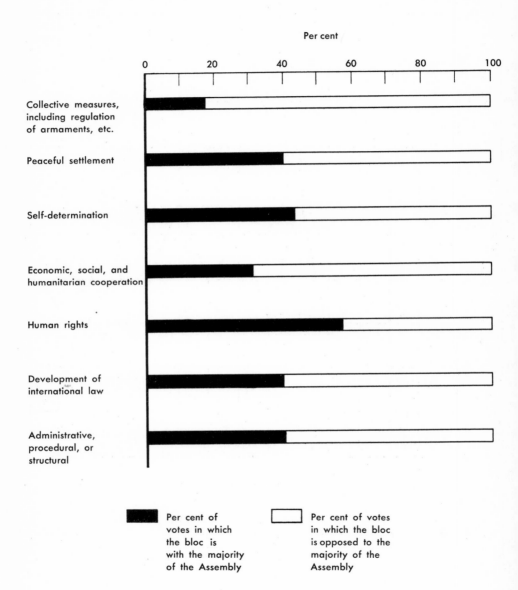

9. Votes of the Soviet bloc in relation to the majority of the General Assembly according to subject categories (percentages based on an adjusted gross number of total roll-call votes)

CHART 10   131

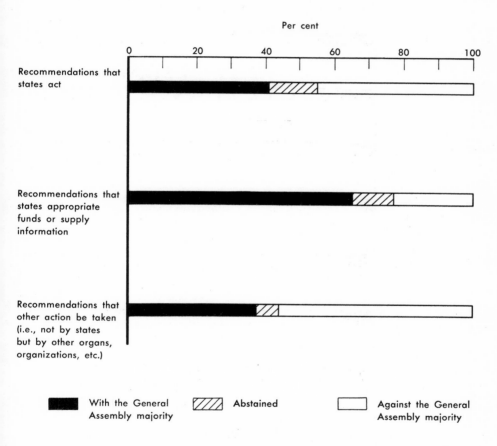

Per cent

Recommendations that
states act

Recommendations that
states appropriate
funds or supply
information

Recommendations that
other action be taken
(i.e., not by states
but by other organs,
organizations, etc.)

With the General   Abstained   Against the General
Assembly majority   Assembly majority

10. Votes of the majority of the members of the Soviet bloc in relation to the votes of the
    majority of the members of the General Assembly, according to the types of recommenda-
    tions involved in the votes (percentages based on an adjusted gross number of roll-call
    votes)

CHART 11

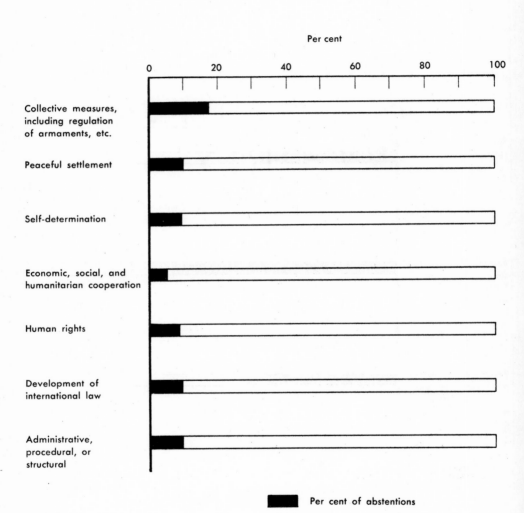

11. Per cent of abstention votes cast by the Soviet bloc according to subject categories (based on an adjusted gross number of roll-call votes)

CHART 12   133

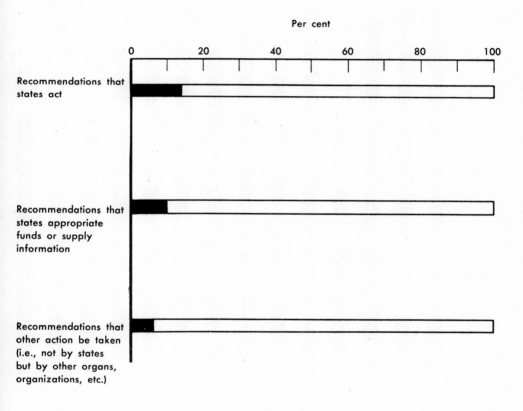

12. Per cent of abstention votes cast by the Soviet bloc according to the types of action (based on an adjusted gross number of roll-call votes)

CHART 13

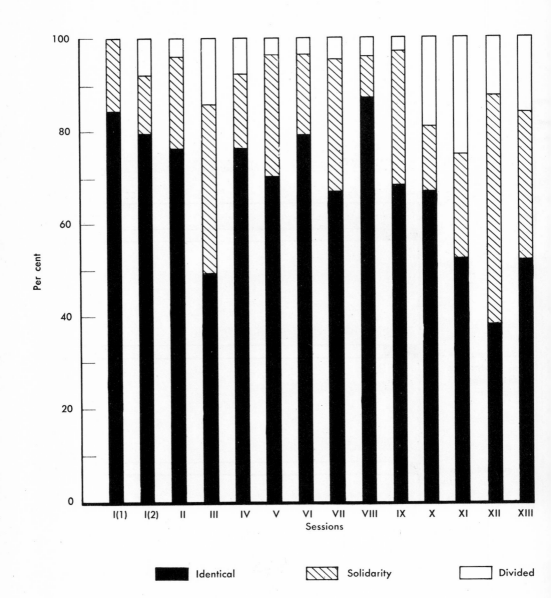

13. Cohesion of the Arab caucusing group as evidenced by the types of votes cast (percentages based on an adjusted gross number of roll-call votes)

CHART 14   135

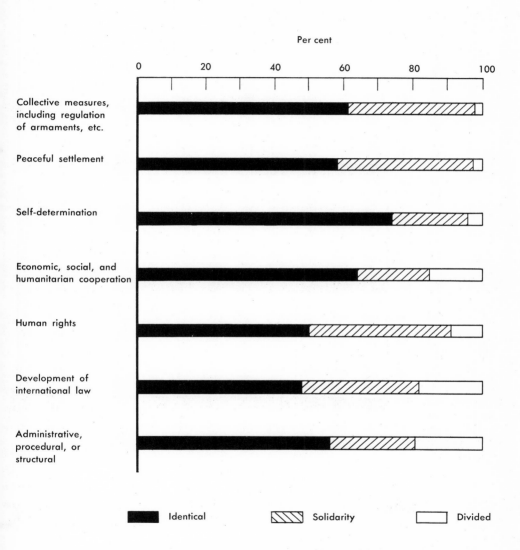

14. Cohesion of the Arab caucusing group according to subjects as evidenced by the types of votes cast (percentages based on an adjusted gross number of roll-call votes)

CHART 15

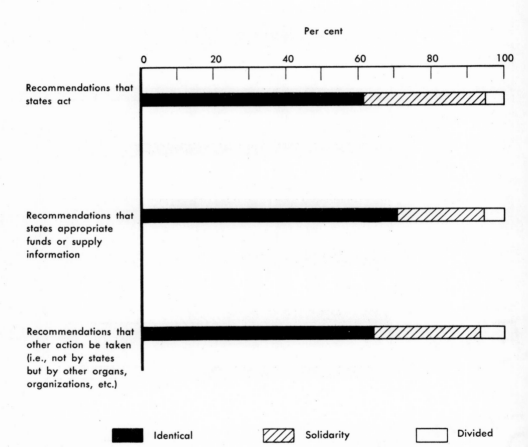

15. Cohesion of the Arab caucusing group according to types of recommendations as evidenced by the types of votes cast (percentages based on an adjusted gross number of roll-call votes)

CHART 16   137

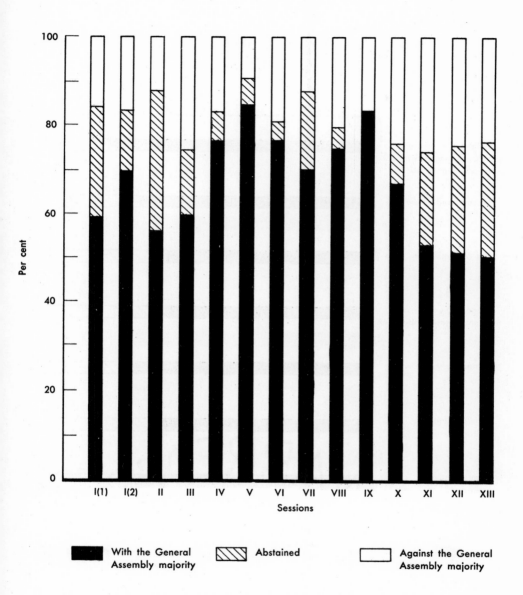

16. Votes of the majority of the members of the Arab caucusing group in relation to the votes of the majority of the members of the General Assembly by sessions (percentages based on an adjusted gross number of roll-call votes)

CHART 17

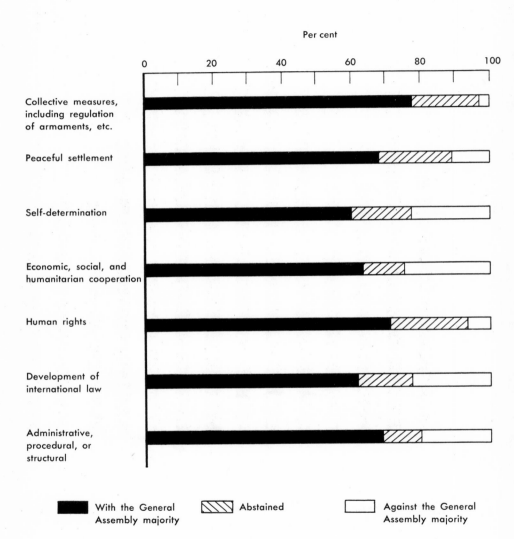

Per cent

17. Votes of the majority of the members of the Arab caucusing group in relation to the votes of the majority of the members of the General Assembly (percentages based on an adjusted gross number of roll-call votes)

CHART 18 139

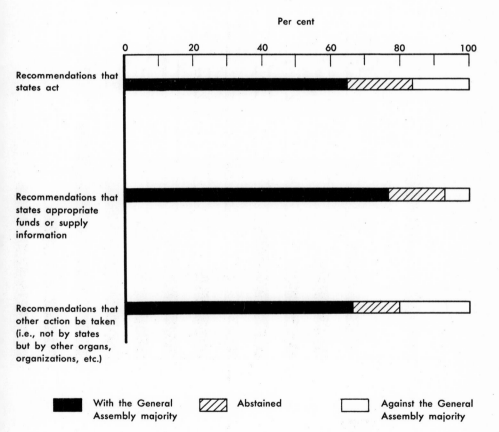

Per cent

Recommendations that states act

Recommendations that states appropriate funds or supply information

Recommendations that other action be taken (i.e., not by states but by other organs, organizations, etc.)

With the General Assembly majority   Abstained   Against the General Assembly majority

18. Votes of the majority of the members of the Arab caucusing group in relation to the votes of the majority of the members of the General Assembly according to the types of recommendations (percentages based on an adjusted gross number of roll-call votes)

CHART 19

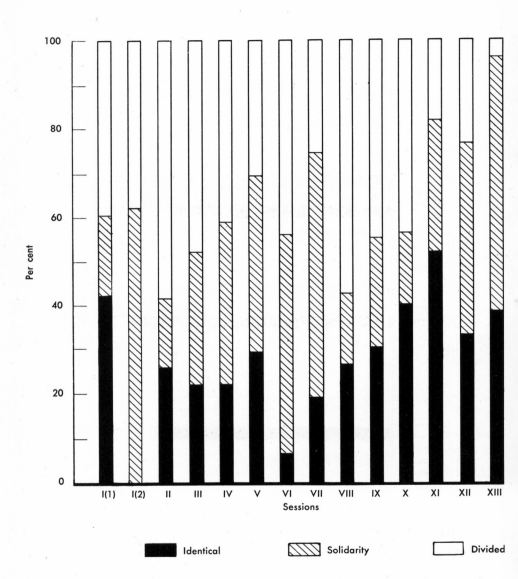

19. Cohesion of the Latin American caucusing group as evidenced by the types of votes cast (percentages based on an adjusted gross number of roll-call votes)

CHART 20

141

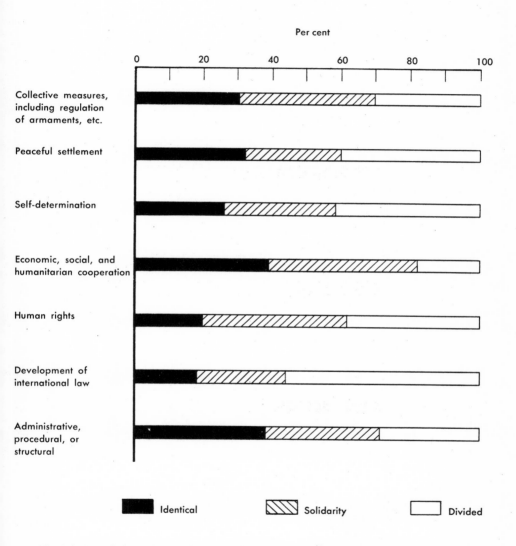

Per cent

Collective measures, including regulation of armaments, etc.

Peaceful settlement

Self-determination

Economic, social, and humanitarian cooperation

Human rights

Development of international law

Administrative, procedural, or structural

■ Identical   ▧ Solidarity   □ Divided

20. Cohesion of the Latin American caucusing group according to types of subjects as evidenced by types of votes cast (percentages based on an adjusted gross number of roll-call votes)

CHART 21

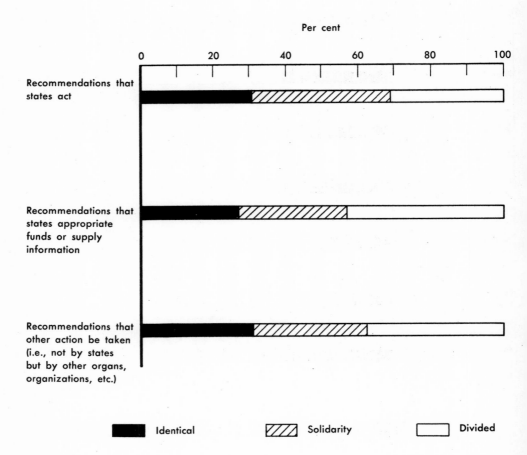

Per cent

Recommendations that
states act

Recommendations that
states appropriate
funds or supply
information

Recommendations that
other action be taken
(i.e., not by states
but by other organs,
organizations, etc.)

Identical   Solidarity   Divided

21. Cohesion of the Latin American caucusing group according to the types of recommenda-
     tions as evidenced by the types of votes cast (percentages based on an adjusted gross
     number of roll-call votes)

CHART 22   **143**

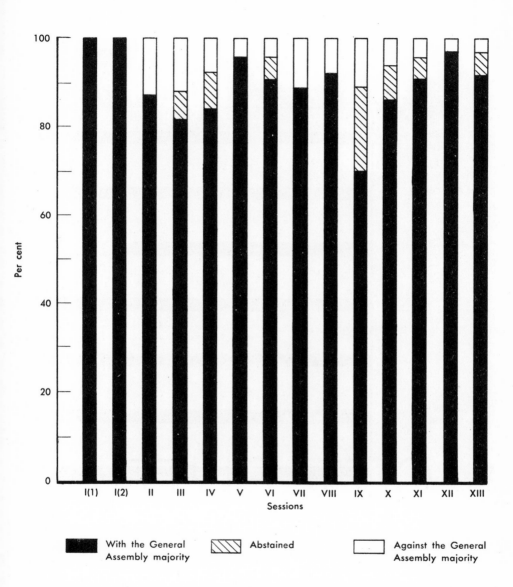

22. Votes of the majority of the members of the Latin American caucusing group in relation to the votes of the majority of the members of the General Assembly by sessions (percentages based on an adjusted gross number of roll-call votes)

CHART 23

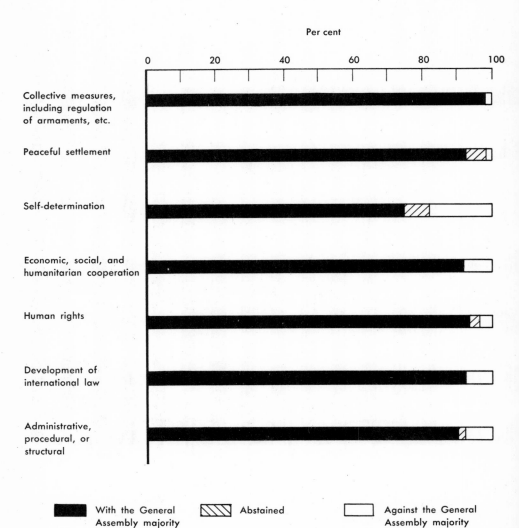

Per cent

Collective measures, including regulation of armaments, etc.

Peaceful settlement

Self-determination

Economic, social, and humanitarian cooperation

Human rights

Development of international law

Administrative, procedural, or structural

With the General Assembly majority

Abstained

Against the General Assembly majority

23. Votes of the majority of the members of the Latin American caucusing group in relation to the votes of the majority of the members of the General Assembly according to types of subjects (percentages based on an adjusted gross number of roll-call votes)

CHART 24   145

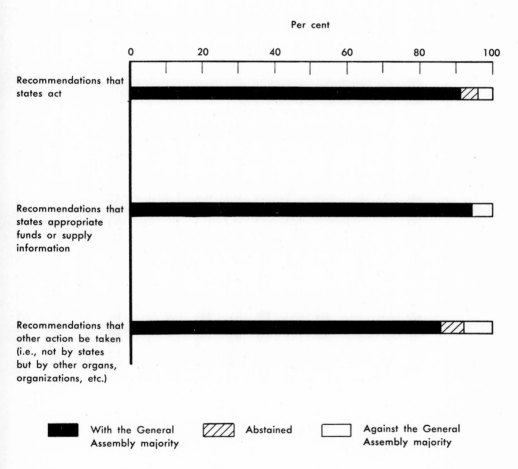

24. Votes of the majority of the members of the Latin American group in relation to the votes of the majority of the members of the General Assembly according to types of recommendations (percentages based on an adjusted gross number of roll-call votes)

CHART 25

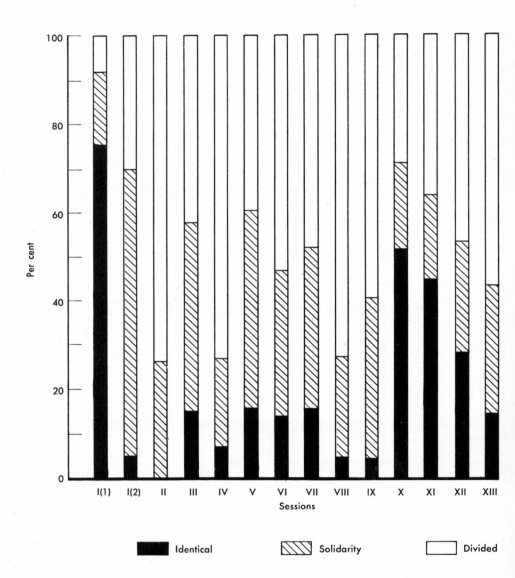

Identical · Solidarity · Divided

25. Cohesion of the Commonwealth caucusing group as evidenced by the types of votes cast (percentages based on an adjusted gross number of roll-call votes)

CHART 26　　　　　　　　　　　　　　　　　　147

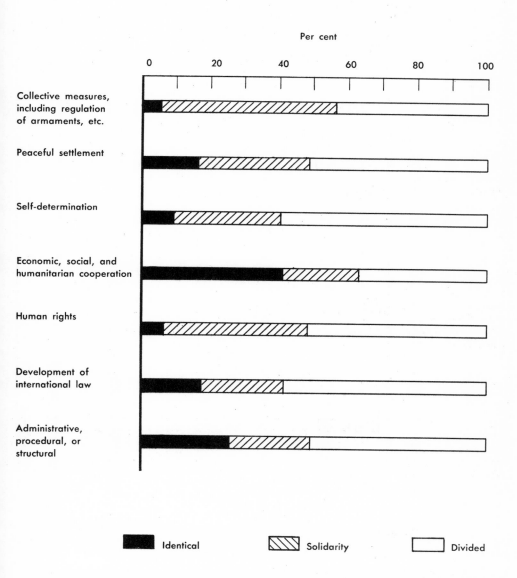

26. Cohesion of the Commonwealth caucusing group according to subjects as evidenced by the types of votes cast (percentages based on an adjusted gross number of roll-call votes)

CHART 27

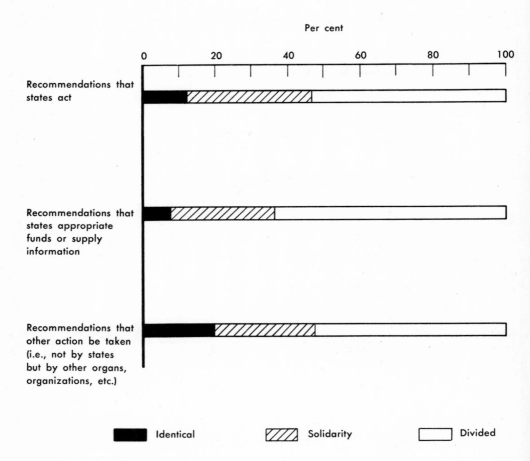

Per cent

Recommendations that
states act

Recommendations that
states appropriate
funds or supply
information

Recommendations that
other action be taken
(i.e., not by states
but by other organs,
organizations, etc.)

Identical   Solidarity   Divided

27. Cohesion of the Commonwealth caucusing group according to the types of recommendations as evidenced by the type of vote (percentages based on an adjusted gross number
of roll-call votes)

CHART 28   149

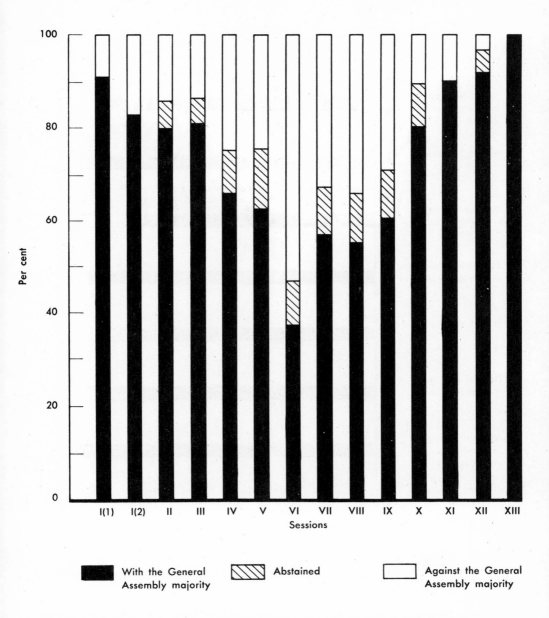

28. Votes of the majority of the members of the Commonwealth caucusing group in relation to the majority of the members of the General Assembly by sessions (percentages based on an adjusted gross number of roll-call votes)

CHART 29

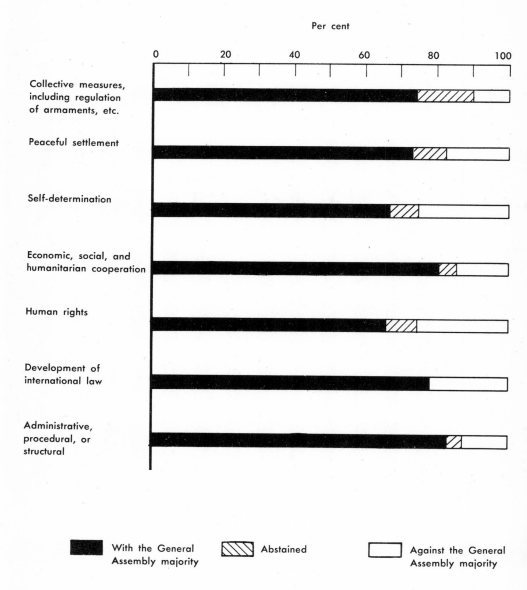

Per cent

29. Votes of the majority of the Commonwealth caucusing group in relation to the votes of the majority of the members of the General Assembly according to types of subjects (percentages based on an adjusted gross number of roll-call votes)

CHART 30   151

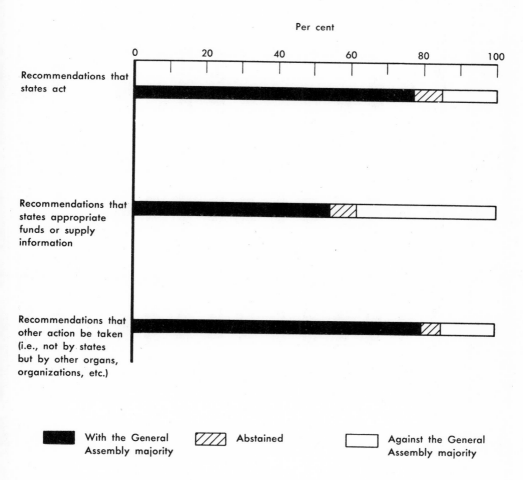

Per cent

0   20   40   60   80   100

Recommendations that
states act

Recommendations that
states appropriate
funds or supply
information

Recommendations that
other action be taken
(i.e., not by states
but by other organs,
organizations, etc.)

With the General   Abstained   Against the General
Assembly majority   Assembly majority

30. Votes of the majority of the members of the Commonwealth caucusing group in relation
to the votes of the majority of the members of the General Assembly according to the
types of recommendations (percentages based on an adjusted gross number of roll-call
votes)

CHART 31

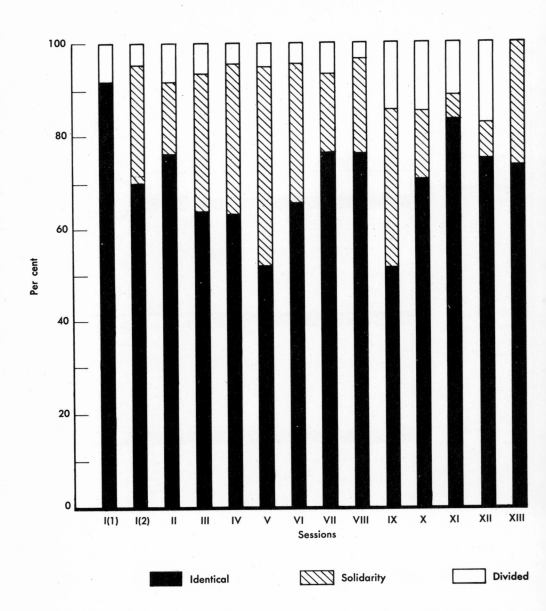

31. Cohesion of the Scandinavian caucusing group as evidenced by the types of votes cast (percentages based on an adjusted gross number of roll-call votes)

CHART 32   153

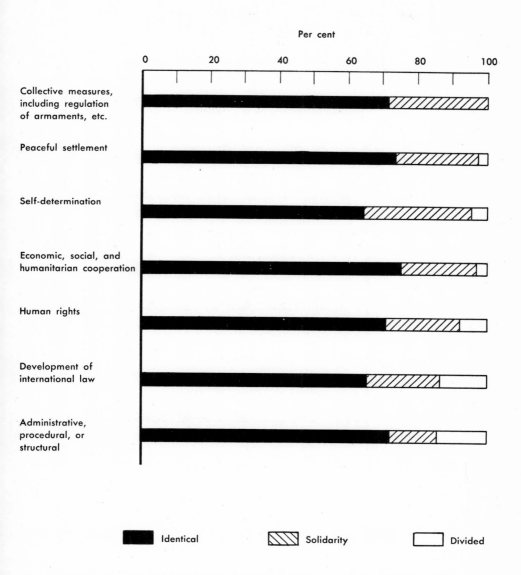

32. Cohesion of the Scandinavian caucusing group according to subject as evidenced by the types of votes cast (percentages based on an adjusted gross number of roll-call votes)

CHART 33

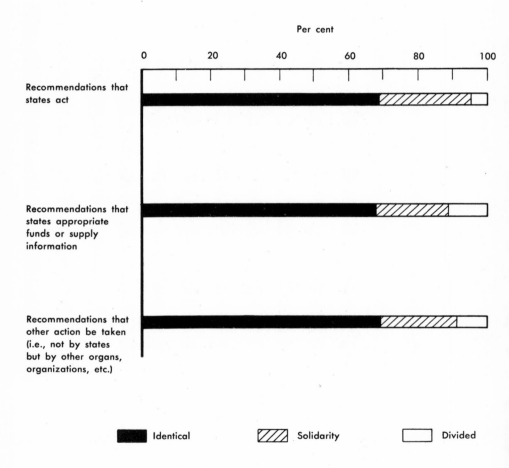

33. Cohesion of the Scandinavian caucusing group according to the types of recommendations as evidenced by the types of votes cast (percentages based on an adjusted gross number of roll-call votes)

CHART 34   155

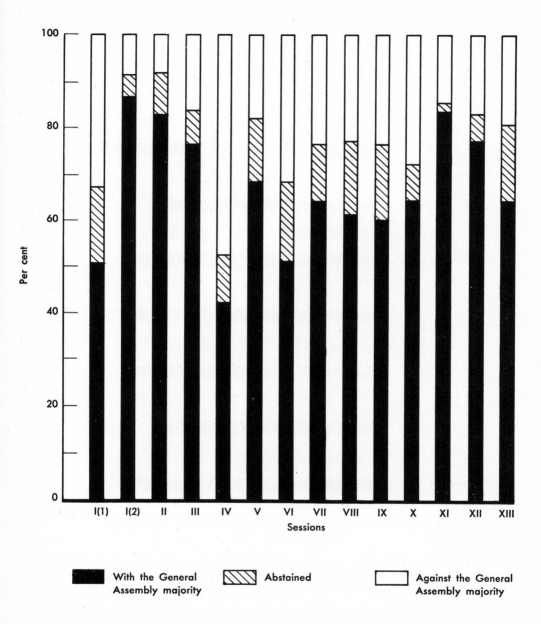

34. Votes of the majority of the members of the Scandinavian caucusing group in relation
to the votes of the majority of the members of the General Assembly by sessions (percentages based on an adjusted gross number of roll-call votes)

CHART 35

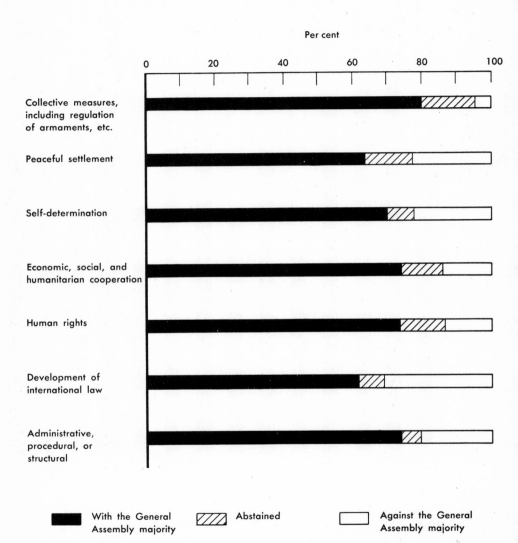

Per cent

35. Votes of the majority of the members of the Scandinavian caucusing group in relation to the votes of the majority of the members of the General Assembly according to types of subjects (percentages based on an adjusted gross number of roll-call votes)

CHART 36   157

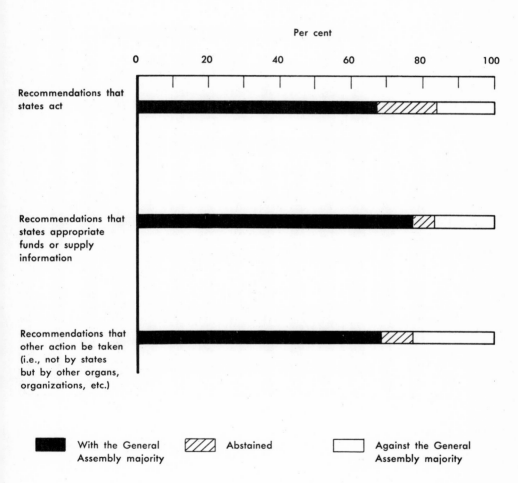

Per cent

36. Votes of the majority of the members of the Scandinavian caucusing group in relation to the votes of the majority of the members of the General Assembly according to types of recommendations (percentages based on an adjusted gross number of roll-call votes)

CHART 37

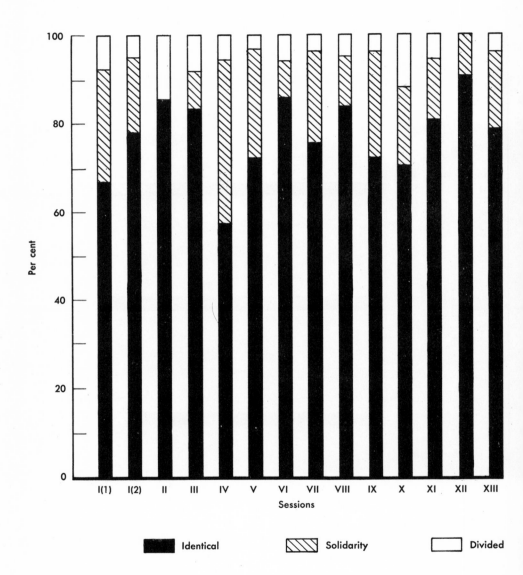

37. Cohesion of the Benelux caucusing group as evidenced by the types of votes cast (percentages based on an adjusted gross number of roll-call votes)

CHART 38   159

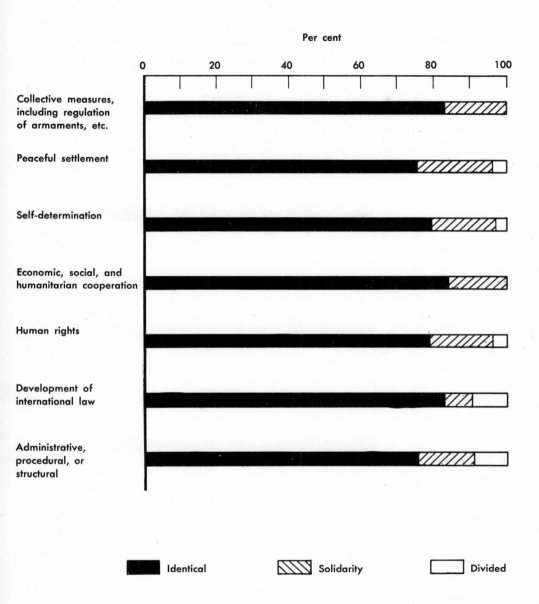

38. Cohesion of the Benelux caucusing group according to subjects as evidenced by the types of votes cast (percentages based on an adjusted gross number of roll-call votes)

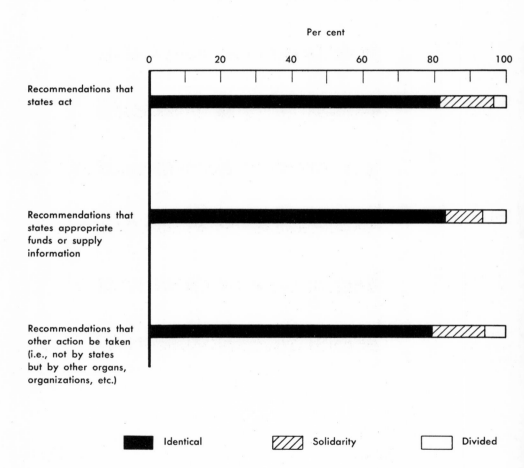

Per cent

0   20   40   60   80   100

Recommendations that
states act

Recommendations that
states appropriate
funds or supply
information

Recommendations that
other action be taken
(i.e., not by states
but by other organs,
organizations, etc.)

■ Identical   ▨ Solidarity   ☐ Divided

39. Cohesion of the Benelux caucusing group according to the types of recommendations as
evidenced by the types of votes cast (percentages based on an adjusted gross number
of roll-call votes)

CHART 40   161

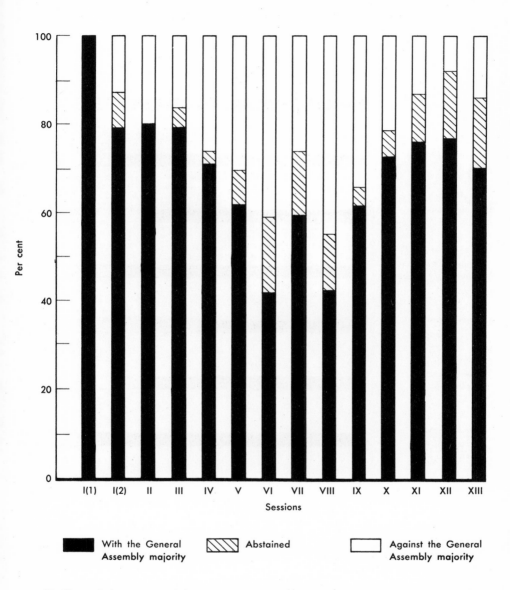

40. Votes of the majority of the members of the Benelux caucusing group in relation to the votes of the majority of the members of the General Assembly by sessions (percentages based on an adjusted gross number of roll-call votes)

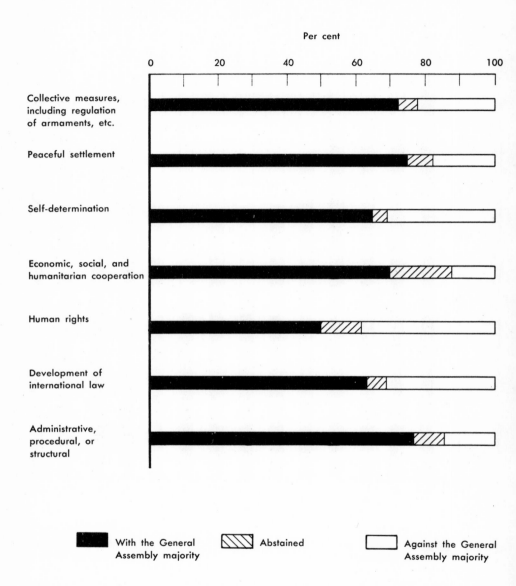

Per cent

Collective measures,
including regulation
of armaments, etc.

Peaceful settlement

Self-determination

Economic, social, and
humanitarian cooperation

Human rights

Development of
international law

Administrative,
procedural, or
structural

■ With the General
Assembly majority   ▨ Abstained   □ Against the General
Assembly majority

41. Votes of the majority of the members of the Benelux caucusing group in relation to the
votes of the majority of the members of the General Assembly according to types of
subjects (percentages are based on an adjusted gross number of roll-call votes)

CHART 42   163

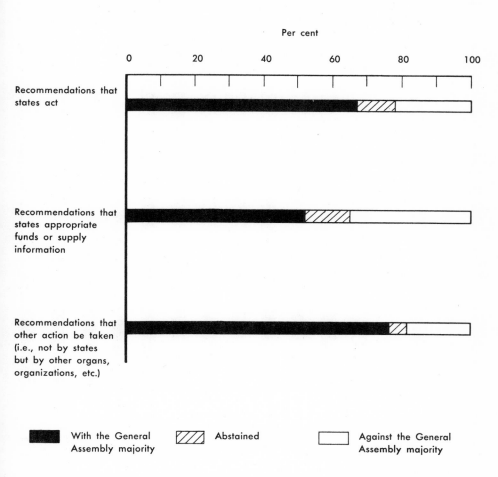

42. Votes of the majority of the members of the Benelux caucusing group in relation to the votes of the majority of the members of the General Assembly according to the types of recommendations (percentages based on an adjusted gross number of roll-call votes)

CHART 43

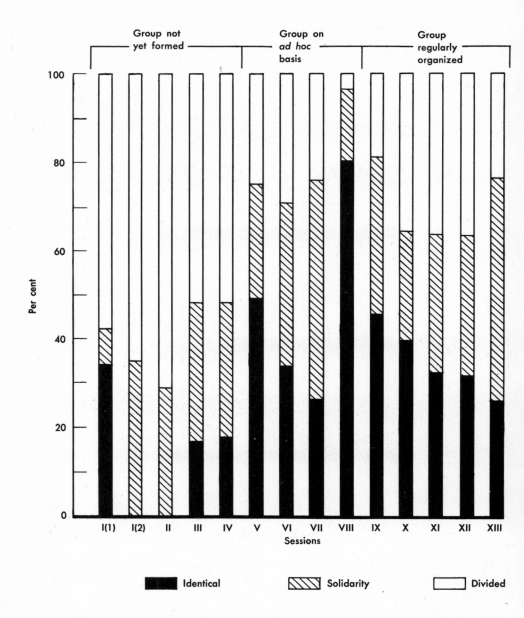

43. Cohesion of the Asian-African caucusing group as evidenced by the types of votes cast (percentages based on an adjusted gross number of roll-call votes)

CHART 44   165

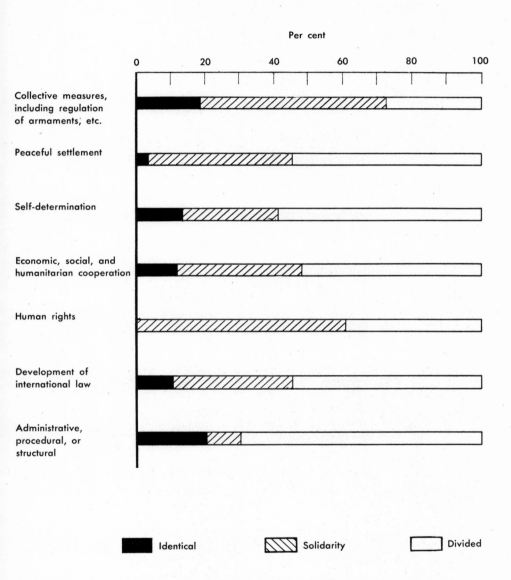

44. Cohesion of the members of the Asian-African caucusing group in the period before the group was operating, as evidenced by the types of votes cast (percentages based on an adjusted gross number of roll-call votes)

CHART 45

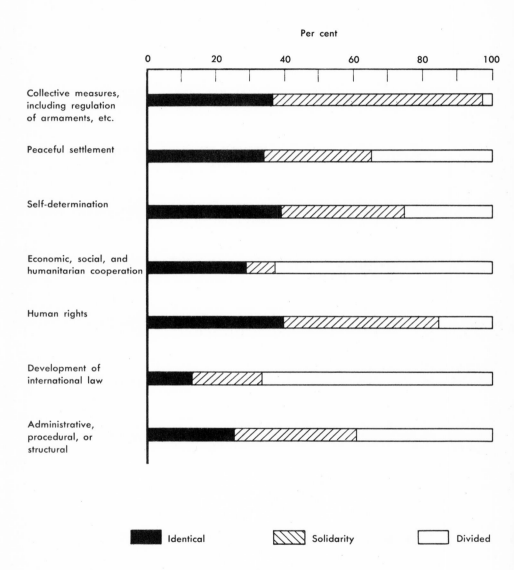

45. Cohesion of the Asian-African caucusing group during the period the group has been operating according to types of subjects as evidenced by the types of votes cast (percentages based on an adjusted gross number of roll-call votes)

CHART 46   167

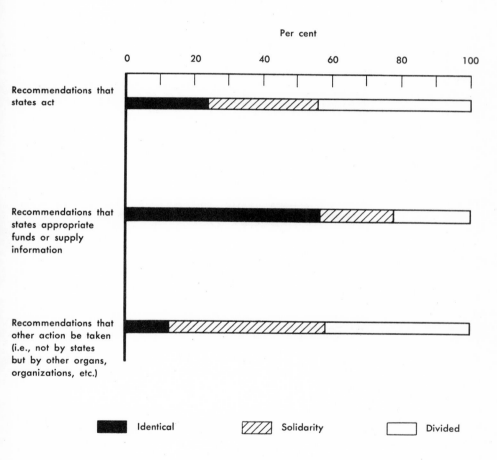

46. Cohesion of the members of the Asian-African caucusing group, in the period before the group operated, according to types of recommendations as evidenced by the types of votes (percentages based on an adjusted gross number of roll-call votes)

CHART 47

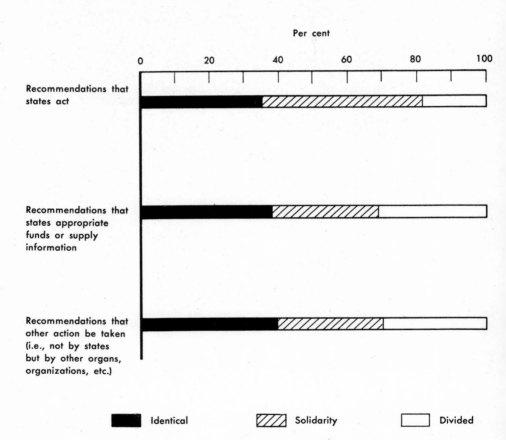

47. Cohesion of Asian-African caucusing group according to the types of recommendations as evidenced by the types of votes (percentages based on an adjusted gross number of roll-call votes)

CHART 48   169

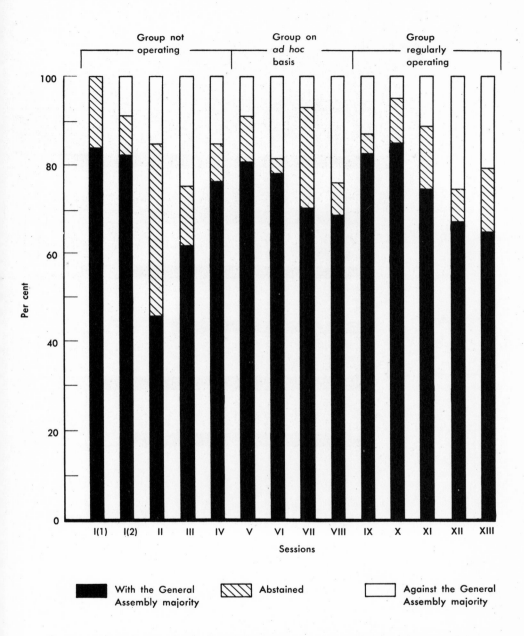

48. Votes of the majority of the Asian-African caucusing group in relation to the votes of the majority of the members of the General Assembly by sessions (percentages based on an adjusted gross number of roll-call votes)

CHART 49

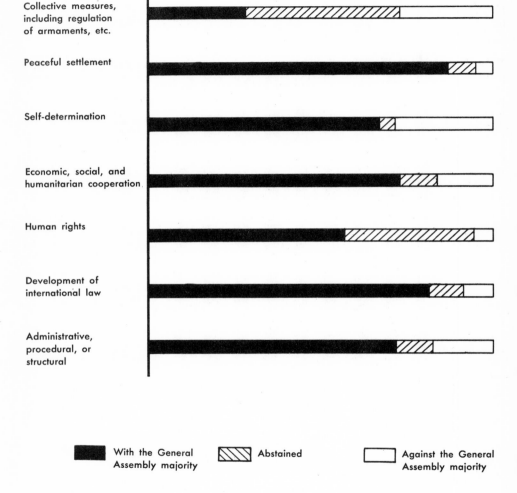

Per cent

49. Votes of the majority of the members of the Asian-African caucusing group, in the period before the group came into being, in relation to the votes of the majority of the members of the United Nations according to types of subjects (percentages based on an adjusted gross number of roll-call votes)

CHART 50   171

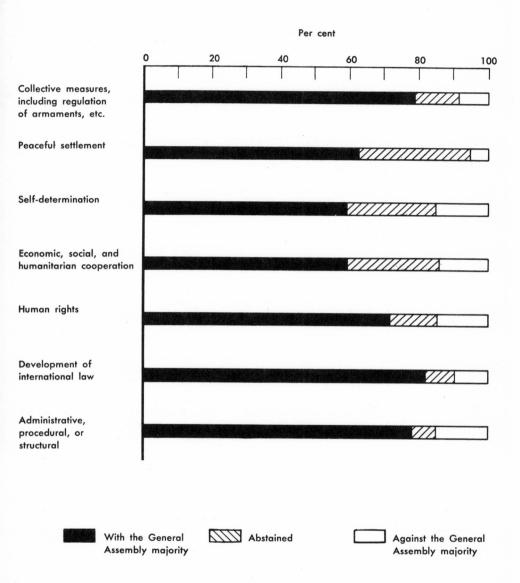

Per cent

Collective measures,
including regulation
of armaments, etc.

Peaceful settlement

Self-determination

Economic, social, and
humanitarian cooperation

Human rights

Development of
international law

Administrative,
procedural, or
structural

■ With the General
Assembly majority

▨ Abstained

□ Against the General
Assembly majority

50. Votes of the majority of the members of the Asian-African caucusing group in relation
to the votes of the majority of the members of the General Assembly according to the
types of subjects (percentages based on an adjusted gross number of roll-call votes)

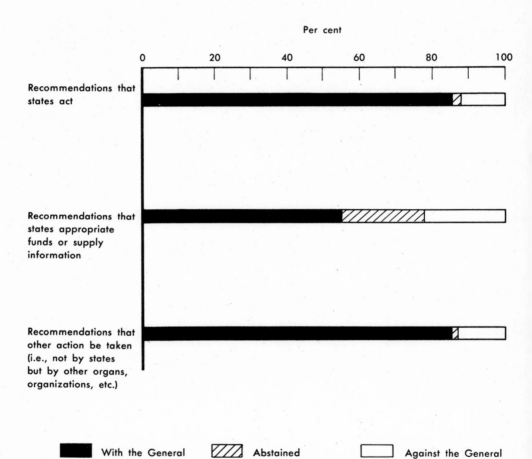

51. Votes of the majority of the members of the Asian-African caucusing group, in the period before the group came into being, in relation to votes of the majority of the members of the General Assembly according to types of recommendations (percentages based on an adjusted gross number of roll-call votes)

CHART 52   173

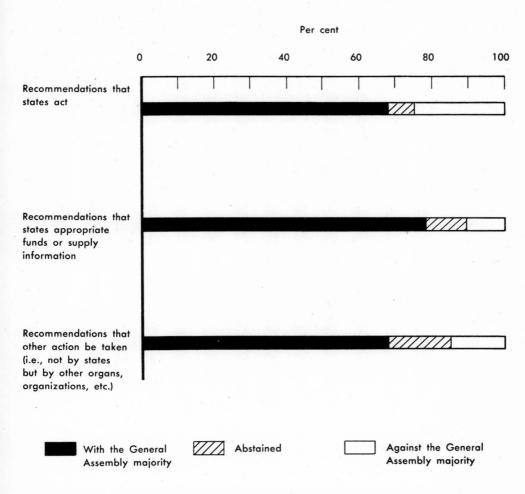

52. Votes of the majority of the members of the Asian-African caucus in relation to the votes of the majority of the members of the General Assembly according to types of recommendations (percentages based on an adjusted gross number of roll-call votes)

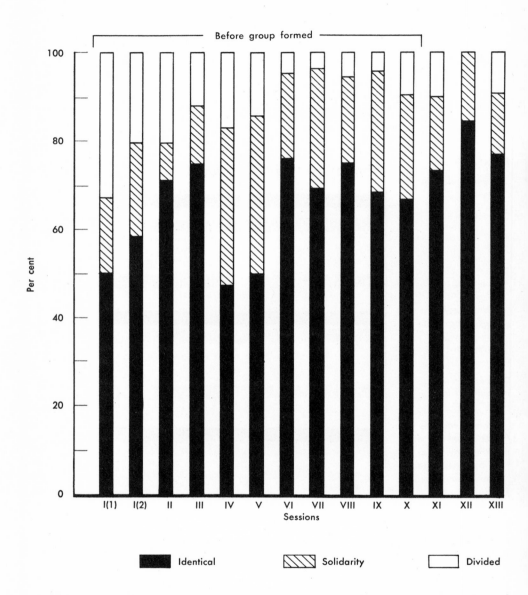

53. Cohesion of the Western European caucusing group as evidenced by the types of votes cast (percentages based on an adjusted gross number of roll-call votes)

CHART 54   175

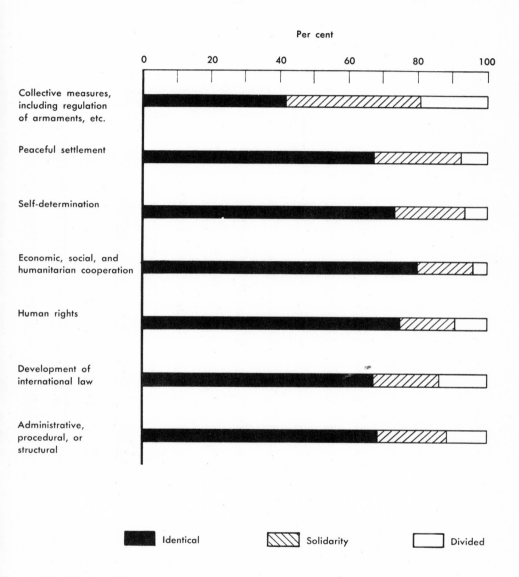

54. Cohesion of the Western European caucus members in the period before the group was organized according to types of subjects (percentages based on an adjusted gross number of roll-call votes)

CHART 55

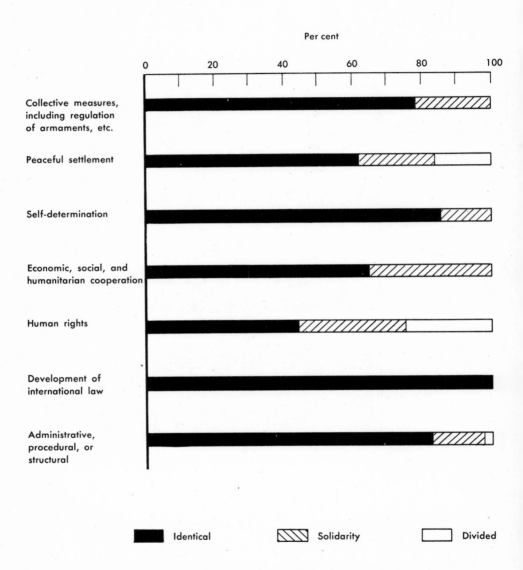

Per cent

55. Cohesion of the Western European caucus according to the types of subjects (percentages based on an adjusted gross number of roll-call votes)

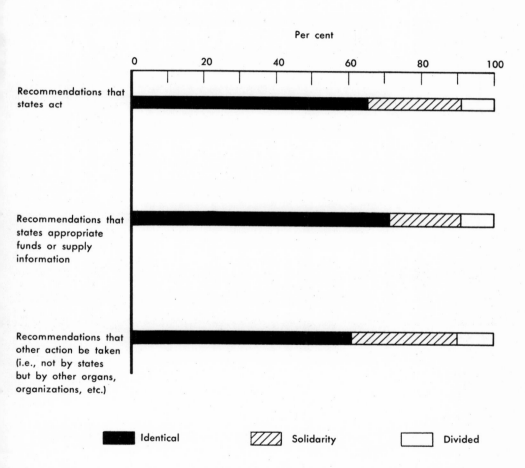

56. Cohesion of the members of the Western European caucus, in the period before the group was formed, according to the types of recommendations as evidenced by the types of votes cast (percentages based on an adjusted gross number of roll-call votes)

CHART 57

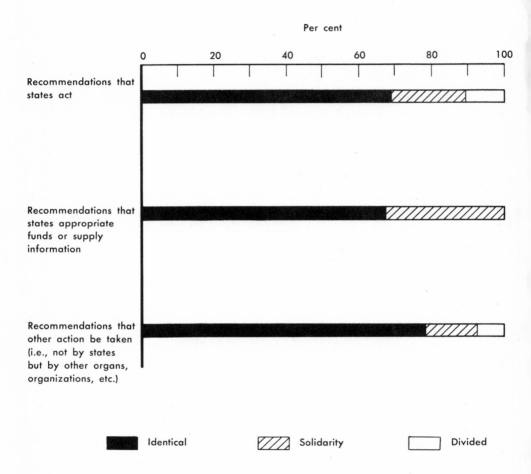

Per cent

0   20   40   60   80   100

Recommendations that
states act

Recommendations that
states appropriate
funds or supply
information

Recommendations that
other action be taken
(i.e., not by states
but by other organs,
organizations, etc.)

■ Identical   ▨ Solidarity   □ Divided

57. Cohesion of the Western European caucusing group according to the types of recommendations as evidenced by the types of votes cast (percentages based on an adjusted gross number of roll-call votes)

CHART 58   179

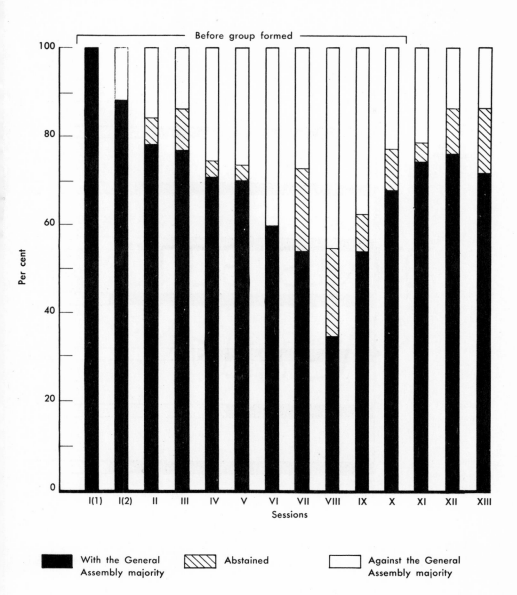

58. Votes of the majority of the Western European caucusing group in relation to the votes of the majority of the members of the General Assembly by sessions (percentages based on an adjusted gross number of roll-call votes)

CHART 59

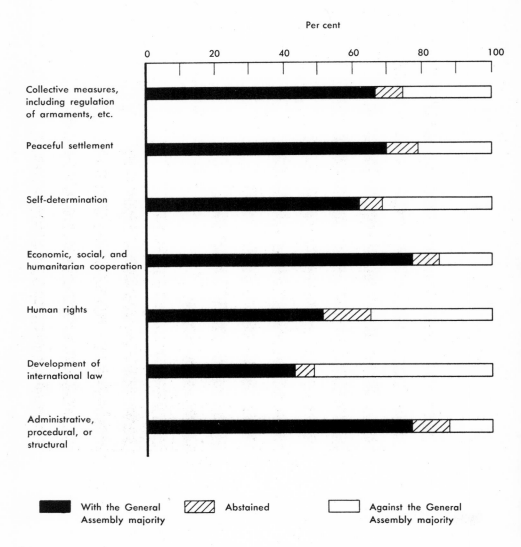

Per cent

59. Votes of the majority of the Western European group members in the period before the group was formed in relation to the votes of the majority of the members of the General Assembly according to the types of subjects (percentages based on an adjusted gross number of roll-call votes)

CHART 60   181

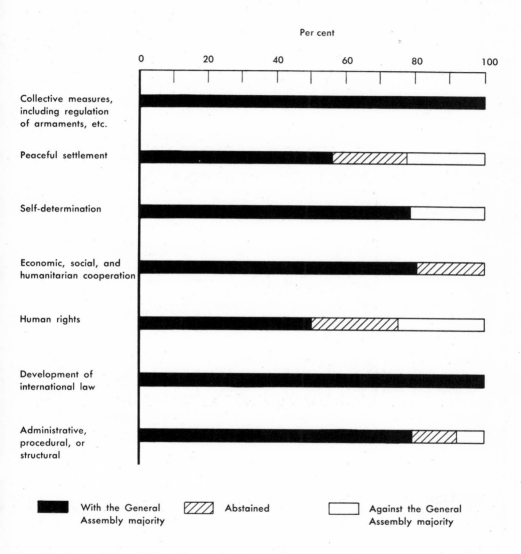

60. Votes of the majority of the members of the Western European caucusing group in relation to the votes of the majority of the members of the General Assembly according to
types of subjects (percentages based on an adjusted gross number of roll-call votes)

CHART 61

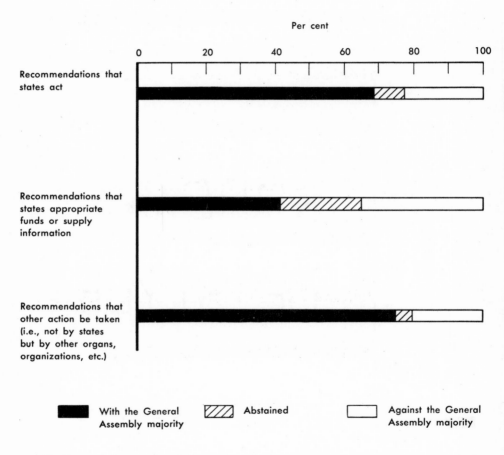

Per cent

61. Votes of the majority of the members of the Western European caucus, in the period before the caucus was formed, in relation to the votes of the majority of the members of the General Assembly according to the types of recommendations (percentages based on an adjusted gross number of roll-call votes)

CHART 62   183

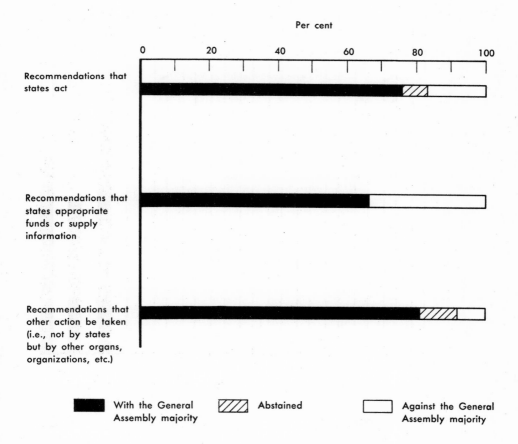

62. Votes of the majority of the members of the Western European caucus in relation to the votes of the majority of the members of the General Assembly according to the types of recommendations (percentages based on an adjusted gross number of roll-call votes)

CHART 63

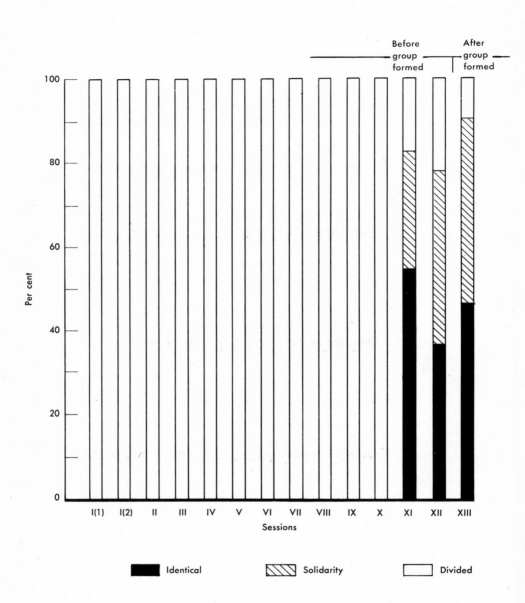

63. Cohesion of the African states as evidenced by the types of votes cast (percentages based on an adjusted gross number of roll-call votes)

CHART 64   185

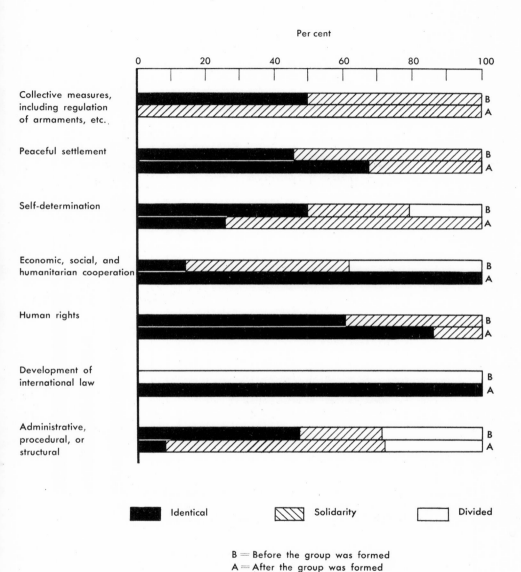

Per cent

64. Cohesion of the African states according to subjects (percentages based on an adjusted gross number of roll-call votes)

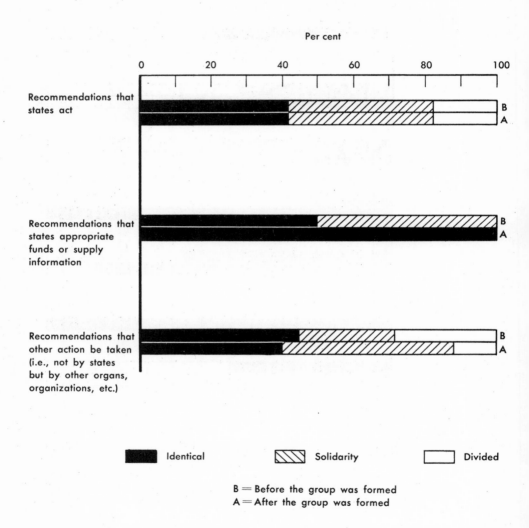

65. Cohesion of the African states according to the types of recommendations (percentages based on an adjusted gross number of roll-call votes)

CHART 66   187

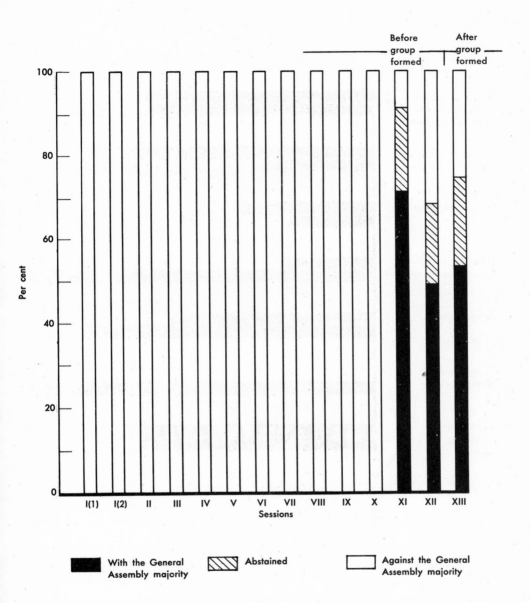

66. Votes of the majority of the African states in relation to the votes of the majority of the General Assembly (percentages based on an adjusted gross number of roll-call votes)

CHART 67

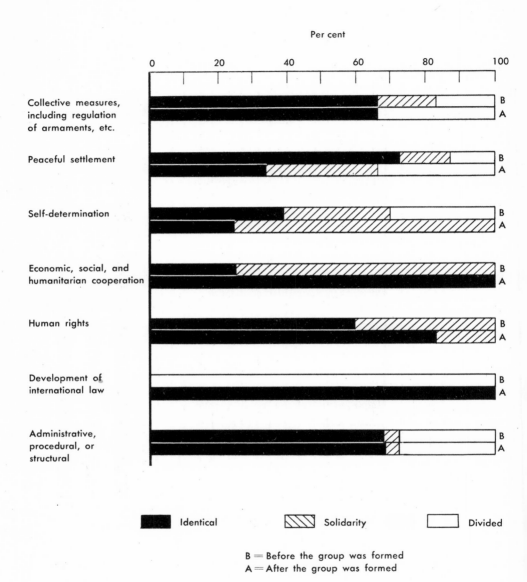

Per cent

67. Votes of the majority of the African states in relation to the votes of the majority of the General Assembly according to the types of subjects (percentages based on an adjusted gross number of roll-call votes)

CHART 68   189

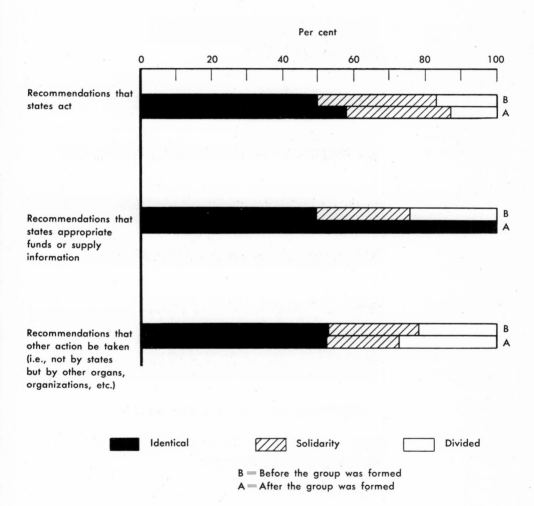

Per cent

68. Votes of the majority of the African states in relation to the votes of the majority of the General Assembly according to the types of recommendations (percentages based on an adjusted gross number of roll-call votes)

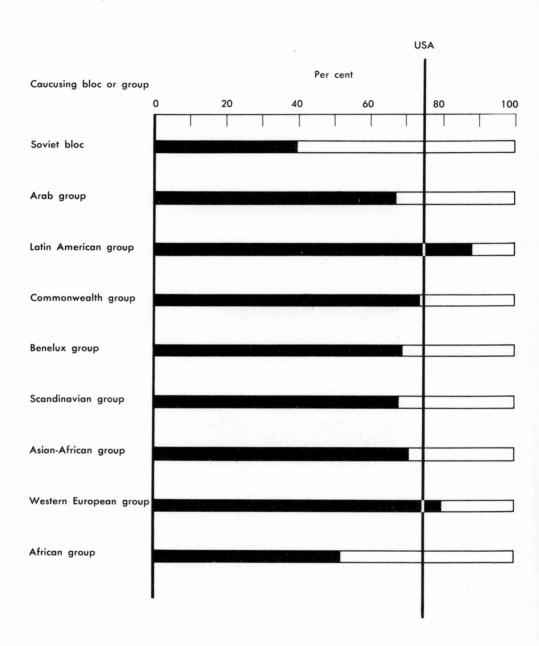

69. Comparison of the degree to which the majority of the various groups tend to vote with the majority of the members of the General Assembly (percentages based on an adjusted gross number of roll-call votes)

CHART 70   191

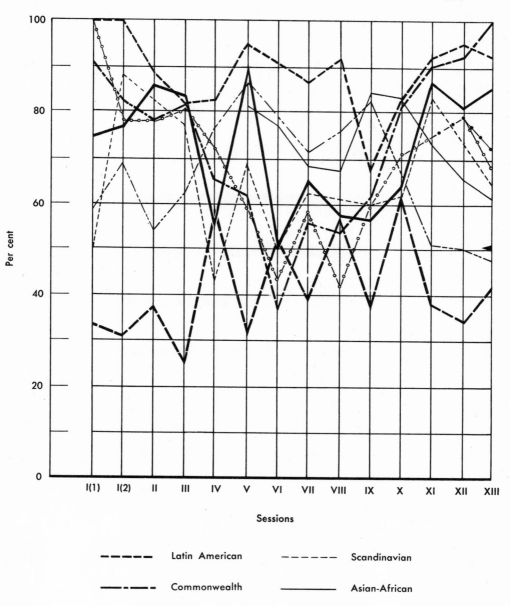

Per cent

Sessions

Latin American   Scandinavian

Commonwealth   Asian-African

USA   ◀ African

Benelux   Arab

Western European   Soviet

70. Comparison of the degree to which the majority of the members of the various groups vote with the majority of the members of the General Assembly session by session (percentages based on an adjusted gross number of roll-call votes)

INDEX

INDEX

Accra Conference group, *see* Conference of Independent African States

Afghanistan, 31, 33, 40, 44, 78, 81, 82–84, 86

African caucusing group, 38, 42, 58, 85, 96, 113, 114; cohesion, 94–95; evolution, 93–94; membership, 31, 94–95; procedures, 94; relationship to U.N. majority, on issues, 106–111, by sessions, 102, 106; voting, degree of solidarity, 95, majority trends, 95

Afro-Asian group, *see* Asian-African caucusing group

Albania, 31, 33, 42, 44, 48, 51

Algeria, 57, 58, 85

Anti-colonial group, 44

Anzus Council group, 40, 97

Arab-Asian group, 79; *see also* Asian-African caucusing group

Arab caucusing group, 38, 43, 46, 68, 78, 85, 86; cohesion, 58–60; evolution, 56; membership, 31, 56–57; procedures, 57–58; relationship to U.N. majority, on issues, 106–111, by sessions, 102–106; voting, degree of solidarity, 61–63, majority trends, 63–64

Arab League group, 40, 43, 56, 58, 59, 80, 86, 96

Arab states group, 44

Argentina, 6, 32, 33, 41, 44, 65, 69

Asian-African caucusing group, 29, 34, 37, 38, 43, 45, 58, 66, 68, 77, 96, 100, 113, 114; cohesion, 85–86; evolution, 78–82; membership, 31, 82–84; procedures, 84–85; relationship to U.N. majority, on issues, 106–111, by sessions, 102, 104–106; voting, degree of solidarity, 87–89, majority trends, 89–90

Asian and African geographical distribution group, 5, 6, 12, 33, 34, 35, 96

Australia, 6, 32, 33, 34, 35, 40, 41, 42, 44, 70, 72, 73, 80, 97

Austria, 1, 32, 33, 35, 41, 44

Baghdad Pact group, 39, 40, 43, 62, 64, 86, 97–98; *see also* Middle East Treaty Organization group

Balkan Alliance group, 40, 98

Bandung Conference group, 40, 43, 78, 81–82, 97

Belgium, 1, 6, 29, 31, 32, 33, 41, 42, 43, 44, 76, 91

Benelux caucusing group, 29, 42, 91, 99; cohesion, 76–77; evolution, 76–77; membership, 31, 76; procedures, 77; relationship to U.N. majority, on issues, 106–111, by sessions, 102–106; voting, degree of solidarity, 77, majority trends, 77–78

Big Three group, 44, 101

Bolivia, 32, 33, 41, 44, 65, 69

Brazil, 6, 32, 33, 41, 44, 65

Brussels Treaty group, *see* Western European Union group

Bulgaria, 31, 33, 42, 44, 48, 50, 51

Burma, 31, 33, 40, 41, 44, 78, 80, 81, 82–84, 85, 86

Byelorussia, 31, 33, 44, 47, 48, 49

Cambodia, 31, 33, 40, 41, 44, 81, 82–84, 86

Canada, 6, 8, 32, 33, 34, 35, 41, 70, 72, 73

Central Treaty Organization group, *see* Baghdad Pact group

Ceylon, 29, 31, 32, 33, 34, 38, 40, 41, 44, 70, 71, 73, 80, 81, 82–84, 85

Chile, 6, 32, 33, 41, 44, 65

China, 32, 33, 35, 44, 50, 75, 79, 81, 86, 87

Colombia, 6, 32, 33, 41, 44, 65

Colombo Plan group, 40, 41

Colonial powers group, 44

Commonwealth caucusing group, 1, 5, 34, 38, 46, 96; cohesion, 71; evolution, 69; membership, 32, 70; procedures, 70–71, 73; relationship to U.N. majority, on issues, 106–111, by sessions, 102–106; voting, degree of solidarity, 71–72, majority trends, 72–73

Commonwealth geographical distribution group, 5, 33, 96

Commonwealth group, 41, 43, 69, 70, 71, 86, 96

Conference of Independent African States, 41, 42–43, 93–94, 96

Costa Rica, 32, 33, 41, 45, 65, 69

BOOKS FROM THE CENTER FOR INTERNATIONAL STUDIES
Massachusetts Institute of Technology

PUBLISHED OR DISTRIBUTED BY HARVARD UNIVERSITY PRESS

The Chinese Family in the Communist Revolution
by C. K. Yang, Technology Press of MIT and Harvard, 1959

A Chinese Village in Early Communist Transition
by C. K. Yang, Technology Press of MIT and Harvard, 1959

The Structure of the East German Economy
by Wolfgang F. Stolper, Harvard, 1960

Bloc Politics in the United Nations
by Thomas Hovet, Jr., Harvard, 1960

FROM OTHER PUBLISHERS

The Dynamics of Soviet Society
by W. W. Rostow, Alfred Levin, et al., Norton, 1953; Mentor Books, 1954

The Prospects for Communist China
by W. W. Rostow, et al., Technology Press of MIT and Wiley, 1954

Soviet Education for Science and Technology
by Alexander G. Korol, Technology Press of MIT and Wiley, 1957

The Economics of Communist Eastern Europe
by Nicolas Spulber, Technology Press of MIT and Wiley, 1957

A Proposal: Key to an Effective Foreign Policy
by M. F. Millikan and W. W. Rostow, Harper, 1957

China's Gross National Product and Social Accounts: 1950–1957
by William W. Hollister, Free Press, 1958

Scratches on Our Minds: American Images of China and India
by Harold R. Isaacs, John Day, 1958

Forging a New Sword: A Study of the Department of Defense
by William R. Kintner, with Joseph I. Coffey and Raymond J. Albright, Harper, 1958

Changing Images of America: A Study of Indian Students' Perceptions
by George V. Coelho, Free Press, 1958

Industrial Change in India: Industrial Growth, Capital Requirements, and Technological Change, 1937–1955
by George Rosen, Free Press, 1958

The American Style: Essays in Value and Performance
edited by Elting E. Morison, Harper, 1958

Handbook for Industry Studies
by Everett E. Hagen, Free Press, 1958

The Japanese Factory: Aspects of Its Social Organization
by James C. Abegglen, Free Press, 1958

The Passing of Traditional Society: Modernizing the Middle East
by Daniel Lerner, with Lucille W. Pevsner (co-sponsored by the Bureau
of Applied Social Research, Columbia University), Free Press, 1958

Industrial Growth in South India: Case Studies in Economic Development
by George B. Baldwin, Free Press, 1959

Financing Economic Development: The Indonesian Case
by Douglas S. Paauw, Free Press, 1960

The Religion of Java
by Clifford Geertz, Free Press, 1960

Postwar Economic Trends in the United States
edited by Ralph E. Freeman, Harper, 1960

The United States in the World Arena
by W. W. Rostow, Harper, 1960

The Question of Government Spending: Public Needs and Private Wants
by Francis M. Bator, Harper, 1960